# THE PAC

## A FUNDAMENTALS-BASED PERCUSSION CURRICULUM

### BY: FRANK CHAPPLE

FOR MORE INFORMATION, PLEASE CONTACT THE PACKET AT:
THEPACKET@VERIZON.NET

YOU CAN ALSO FOLLOW THE PACKET ON FACEBOOK, INSTAGRAM, AND TWITTER.

# Acknowledgements

The Packet is dedicated to all of my past, current and future students who continue to inspire and teach me everyday...

Thank you to all my colleagues and mentors who helped shape my teaching career: Marty Hurley, Mark McGahey, Lee Beddis, Lee Smith, David Puckett, JJ Pipitone, Russell Wharton, Jed Maus, Cristian Alcocer and many others.

Thank you Ryan Heath for the great work on the cover photography and design.

A very special thank you to my daughter, Avery, for her patience and support while I completed this project.

# THE PACKET

## TABLE OF CONTENTS

- Introduction

- Section 1: Rhythm

- Section 2: Chops

- Section 3: Rudiments

- Section 4: Mallets

- Section 5: Drumset

- Section 6: Assignments Charts

# THE PACKET

Hello,

The packet that you are holding is the curriculum that establishes a strong foundation for all percussion students. The purpose of *The Packet* is to set every student on the path to becoming a complete percussionist. This packet will work the fundamentals of 5 essential areas of the percussion foundation:

1. Rhythm
2. Chops
3. Rudiments
4. Mallets: 2 and 4 mallet technique
5. Drumset.

It is my hope that through *The Packet*, along with a strong supplementation of solo and ensemble literature, instructional method books, advanced level etudes, participation in a wide variety of performing ensembles, weekly private lessons and a consistent individual practice regimen, that you will be set to have an enjoyable and lifelong musical journey. How far this journey goes is entirely up to YOU...

Let's get started!!!

*Frank Chapple*

Frank Chapple

# THE PACKET
## COUNTING SYSTEM

The Packet Counting System is a defined method of counting variations designed to develop the student's rhythmic vocabulary and tempo control. By utilizing a variety of counting strategies, the student's internalization of pulse, rhythms recognition, and sight-reading speed and accuracy can be greatly increased.

The counting variations listed below are not in a specific order. All of the variations should be utilized in group rehearsals as well as individual practice sessions. Since each counting variation has its own strengths (and weaknesses) it is important that the student be able to master all of them.

All counting variations must be performed *OUT LOUD*. There is no "counting in your head". If the counting is not vocalized then the counting variation has not been mastered...

## COUNTING VARIATIONS

1: *COUNT EVERYTHING*
   -The student will count everything on the page
   -Notes and Rests are treating equally and are counted with the same volume and intensity
   -Variation strengths:
      1. teaches the importance of the value of the rest
      2. teaches the student to "see" the entirety of the measure
      3. teaches the student to keep track of each beat in the measure

*EXAMPLE 1*

|   |    |    |   |    |   |   |    |    |   |   |   |    |    |   |    |   |
|---|----|----|---|----|---|---|----|----|---|---|---|----|----|---|----|---|
| 1 | TE | TA | 2 | TE | 3 |   | 4  | TI | TA | 1 |   | 2 | 3 | LA | LEE | 4 | TE | 1 |
| 1 | &  | AH | 2 | &  | 3 |   | 4  | E  | AH | 1 |   | 2 | 3 | LA | LEE | 4 | &  | 1 |

# THE PACKET
## COUNTING SYSTEM

### 2: *COUNT WHAT YOU HEAR*

-THE PERFORMER WILL COUNT OUT LOUD ONLY THE "PLAYED NOTES" ON THE PAGE

-ALL RESTS ARE INTERNALIZED AND ARE HEARD AS SILENCE

-<u>VARIATION STRENGTHS</u>:

1. TEACHES THE ABILITY TO HEAR WHAT IS BEING PLAYED

2. TEACHES THE ABILITY TO SELF-ANALYZE DURING PRACTICE SESSIONS AND BE ABLE TO KNOW WHEN SOMETHING IS PLAYED CORRECTLY OR INCORRECTLY

3. TEACHES THE ABILITY TO INTERNALIZE THE RESTS

*EXAMPLE 2*

### 3: *COUNT THE DOWNBEATS (FOOT TAP)*

-THE STUDENT WILL ONLY COUNT THE BEATS OR FOOT TAP

-THIS CAN BE ADJUSTED FOR COMPLEX TIME SIGNATURES

-<u>VARIATION STRENGTHS</u>:

1. TEACHES THE STUDENT TO FOCUS ON THE PULSE (TEMPO) OF THE MUSIC

2. TEACHES THE RELATIONSHIP BETWEEN THE RHYTHMS AND THE PULSE

3. IMPROVES COORDINATION BETWEEN THE FOOT TAP AND THE HANDS

4. DEVELOPS THE "FEEL" OF THE MUSIC INSTEAD OF JUST RHYTHMIC ACCURACY

5. IS MORE CHALLENGING THAN IT SEEMS

*EXAMPLE 3*

# THE PACKET
## Counting System

### 4: COUNT THE SUBDIVISIONS
-The student will count the subdivisions for all notes
and rests
-Variations strengths:
1. teaches the ability to recognize and control
the space between notes
2. Teaches the ability to articulate rhythms at a
faster tempo
3. teaches pulse control (especially for slower
rhythms)

### EXAMPLE 4-A

ORIGINAL RHYTHM

RHYTHM SUBDIVISIONS

### EXAMPLE 4-B

SUBDIVISIONS COUNTING

1 TI TE TA 2 TI TE TA 3    TE    4 TI TE TA    1    TE    2    TE    3 LA LEE 4 TI TE TA    1
1 E & AH 2 E & AH 3    &    4 E & AH    1    &    2    &    3 LA LEE 4 E & AH    1

### EXAMPLE 4-C

ORIGINAL RHYTHM W/ SUBDIVISIONS COUNTING

1 TI TE TA 2 TI TE TA 3    TE    4 TI TE TA    1 TE    2    TE    3 LA LEE 4 TI TE TA 1
1 E & AH 2 E & AH 3    &    4 E & AH    1 &    2    &    3 LA LEE 4 E & AH 1

# THE PACKET
## LEARNING PROCESS

THE PACKET LEARNING PROCESS IS A DEFINED SYSTEM DESIGNED TO EXPEDITE THE INDIVIDUAL PRACTICE TIME NEEDED TO SUCCESSFULLY MASTER ANY NEW MUSIC OR SKILL. THIS PROCESS IS DIVIDED INTO TWO CATEGORIES:

1. DRUMMING MUSIC/SKILLS

2. *MALLET MUSIC/SKILLS

*THE MALLET MUSIC CATEGORY WILL WORK FOR ANY MUSIC THAT REQUIRES A VARIETY OF PITCHES, PLAYING SURFACES, ETC. THIS WOULD INCLUDE 2-MALLETS, 4-MALLETS, AND TIMPANI.

ALL STEPS MUST BE MASTERED BEFORE MOVING TO THE NEXT ONE. NO SKIPPING STEPS!!!!

## DRUMMING PROCESS

### STEP 1: COUNTING ONLY
- COUNT ALL RHYTHMS OUT LOUD (SKELETONS ONLY)
- TEMPO IS MUCH SLOWER THAN PERFORMANCE TEMPO
- ALL DYNAMICS (HEIGHTS) ARE PRESENT

### STEP 2: AIR DRUMMING
- COUNT ALL RHYTHMS OUT LOUD (SKELETONS ONLY)
- TEMPO IS MUCH SLOWER THAN PERFORMANCE TEMPO
- ALL DYNAMICS (HEIGHTS) ARE PRESENT
- ADD "AIR DRUMMING" (CORRECT STICKINGS)

### STEP 3: PLAYING WITH SKELETONS
- COUNT ALL RHYTHMS OUT LOUD (SKELETONS ONLY)
- TEMPO IS MUCH SLOWER THAN PERFORMANCE TEMPO
- ALL DYNAMICS (HEIGHTS) ARE PRESENT
- PLAY RHYTHMS AND RUDIMENTS (SKELETONS ONLY)

### STEP 4: PLAYING AS WRITTEN
- COUNT ALL RHYTHMS OUT LOUD (SKELETONS ONLY)
- TEMPO IS MUCH SLOWER THAN PERFORMANCE TEMPO
- ALL DYNAMICS (HEIGHTS) ARE PRESENT
- PLAY ALL RHYTHMS AND RUDIMENTS (AS WRITTEN)

### STEP 5: PERFORMANCE LEVEL PLAYING
- ALL COUNTING IS INTERNALIZED
- PERFORMANCE TEMPOS
- PLAY RHYTHMS/RUDIMENTS AS WRITTEN

# THE PACKET
# LEARNING PROCESS

## MALLET/TIMPANI PROCESS

### STEP 1: SAY IT
- SAY OUT LOUD THE NAMES OF THE NOTES (PITCHES)
- NO TEMPO IS PRESENT
- CORRECT DYNAMICS ARE PRESENT

### STEP 2: SAY IT WITH TEMPO
- SAY OUT LOUD THE NAMES OF THE NOTES (PITCHES)
- CORRECT DYNAMICS ARE PRESENT
- **SLOW TEMPO AND RHYTHMS ARE PRESENT**

### STEP 3: FIND IT
- SAY OUT LOUD THE NAMES OF THE NOTES (PITCHES)
- SLOW TEMPO AND RHYTHM ARE PRESENT
- CORRECT DYNAMICS ARE PRESENT
- **TOUCH THE CORRECT BAR FOR EACH NOTE**

### STEP 4: *AIR IT
- SAY OUT LOUD THE NAMES OF THE NOTES (PITCHES)
- SLOW TEMPO AND RHYTHM ARE PRESENT
- CORRECT DYNAMICS ARE PRESENT
- **AIR DRUM OVER THE CORRECT BARS (CORRECT STICKINGS)**

### STEP 5: PLAY IT
- SAY OUT LOUD THE NAMES OF THE NOTES (PITCHES)
- SLOW TEMPO AND RHYTHM ARE PRESENT
- CORRECT DYNAMICS ARE PRESENT
- **PLAY THE INSTRUMENT**

### STEP 6: PERFORM IT
- NOTE NAMES ARE INTERNALIZED
- TEMPO AND RHYTHMS ARE PERFORMANCE TEMPO
- CORRECT DYNAMICS ARE PRESENT


*WHEN PRACTICING 4 MALLETS, STEP 4 WILL BECOME THE PLAY ON FLOOR PORTION OF THE PROCESS. THIS STEP INCLUDES:

- SLOW TEMPO AND RHYTHMS

- CORRECT STICKINGS

- PROPER 4 MALLET TECHNIQUE

# THE PACKET
## HEIGHTS CHART

>THIS HEIGHTS CHART IS USED FOR ALL RUDIMENTAL (OUTDOOR) DRUMMING.

>WE DO NOT USE THIS CHART WHEN PERFORMING CONCERT STYLE (INDOOR) LITERATURE. HEIGHTS FOR CONCERT DRUMMING SHOULD BE ADJUSTED APPROPRIATELY FOR THE ENSEMBLE.

| DYNAMIC | NAME | VOLUME | HEIGHT |
|---------|------|--------|--------|
| PP | PIANISSIMO | VERY SOFT | 1.5" |
| P | PIANO | SOFT | 3" |
| MP | MEZZO PIANO | MEDIUM SOFT | 6" |
| MF | MEZZO FORTE | MEDIUM LOUD | 9" |
| F | FORTE | LOUD | 12" |
| FF | FORTISSIMO | VERY LOUD | 15" |

# SECTION ONE

# RHYTHM

# Rhythm Sheets
# Sticking Variations

The following sticking variations should be applied to all rhythm sheets. Once this list has been mastered, feel free to "invent" your own stickings that will challenge you and expand your vocabulary.

### *Variation 1: Right Hand Lead

R L R L R  L R L R R  R L R L R  L R L R R  R L R L  L R L R

### Variation 2: Left Hand Lead

L R L R L  R L R L L  L R L R L  R L R L L  L R L R  R L R L

### Variation 3: Right Hand Unlead (Alternating)

R L R L R L  R L R L R L  R L R L R L  R L R L R L  L R L R

### Variation 4: Left Hand Unlead (Alternating)

L R L R L R  L R L R L R  L R L R L R  L R L R L R  R L R L

### Variation 5: Right Hand Lead Doubles (Diddles)

R R L L R  L R R L R  L L R L R  R L R R L  L R L L R

### Variation 6: Left Hand Lead Doubles (Diddles)

L L R R L  R L L R L  R R L R L  L R L L R  R L R R L

### Variation 7: Right Hand Lead Inverts

R L L R R L  L R R L L R  L R R L R L  R L L R L L  R R

### Variation 8: Left Hand Lead Inverts

L R R L L R  R L L R R L  R L L R L R  L R R L R R  L L

## *All rhythm sheets are labeled with the RH Lead Sticking

©FECIV

# RHYTHM SHEET:
## QUARTER NOTES/RESTS

*1-1*

# Rhythm Sheet:
## Half Notes/Rests

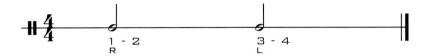

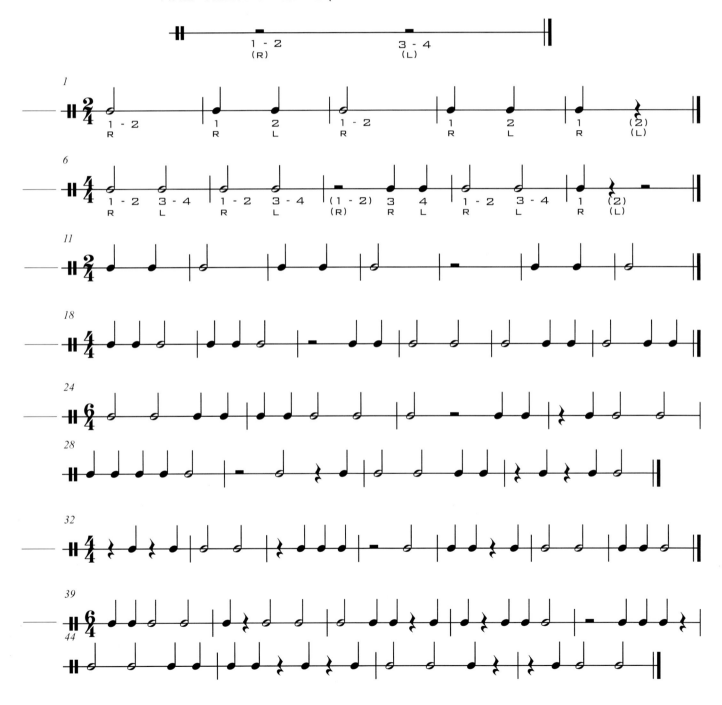

# Rhythm Sheet:
## Whole Notes/Rests

*Whole Note*: 1 Note equals 4 Beats

*Whole Rest*: 1 Rest equals 4 Beats

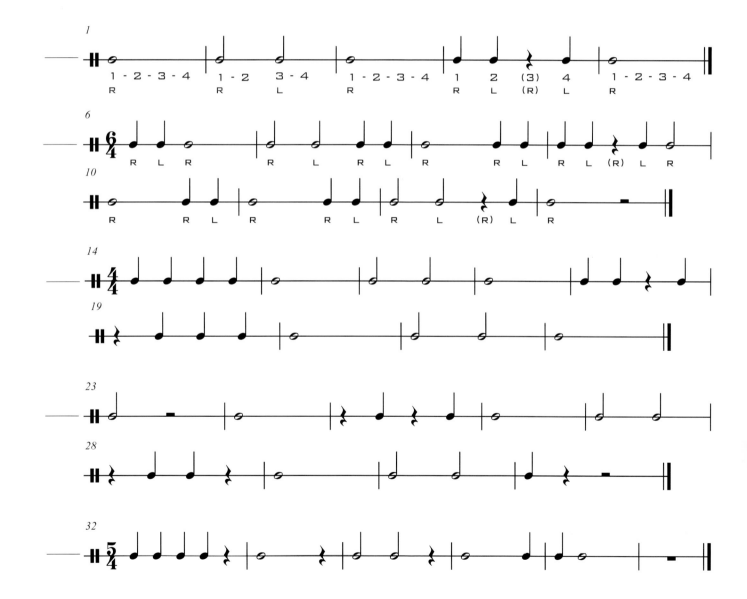

1-3

# RHYTHM SHEET:

## WHOLE, HALF AND QUARTERS

### LOOK OUT FOR THE REPEAT SIGNS!!!!

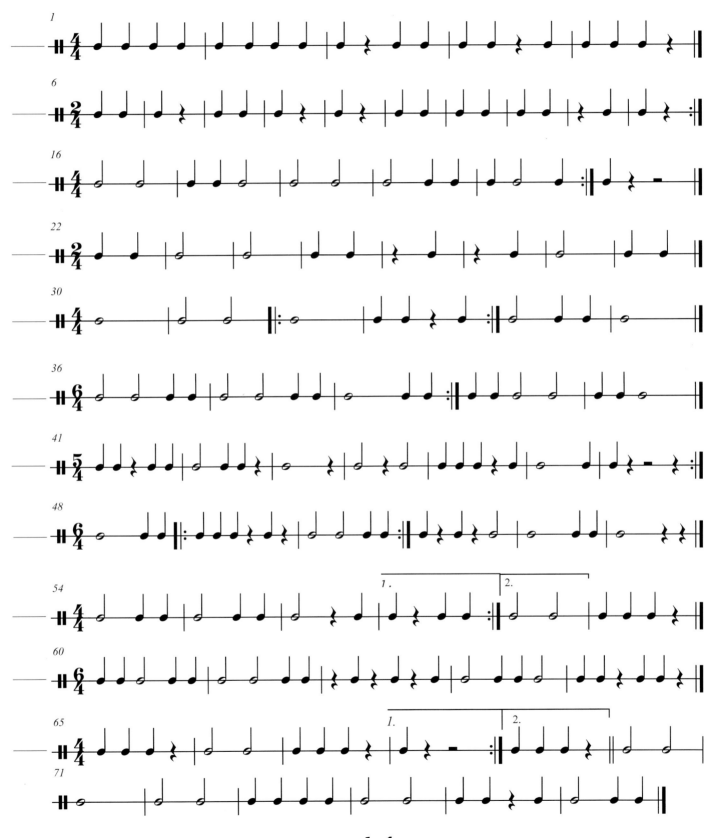

*1-4*

# RHYTHM SHEET:
## 8TH NOTES

*8TH NOTE*: 2 NOTES PER 1 BEAT ---- ONE 8TH NOTE EQUALS 1/2 A BEAT

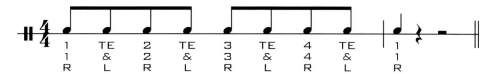

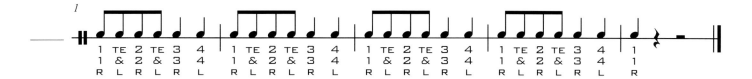

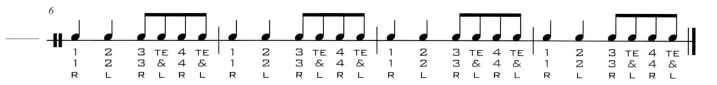

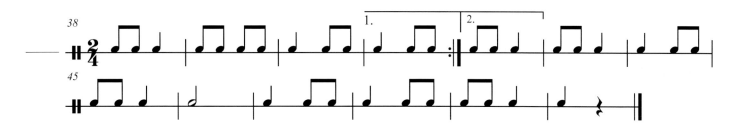

*1-5*

# RHYTHM SHEET:
## MORE 8TH NOTES...

# RHYTHM SHEET:
## ADDING DYNAMICS

## REFER TO THE HEIGHTS CHART IN THE INTRO SECTION

# Rhythm Sheet:
## 8th Notes w/ Rests

### 8th rests on upbeats (TE/&'s)

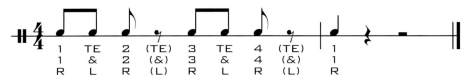

### 8th rests on downbeats (#'s)

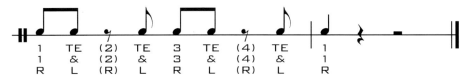

# RHYTHM SHEET:
## MORE 8TH RESTS...

*1-9*

# RHYTHM SHEET:
## DOTTED NOTES

### DOTTED WHOLE NOTE - 6 BEATS

### DOTTED HALF NOTE - 3 BEATS

### DOTTED QUARTER NOTE - 1 AND 1/2 BEATS

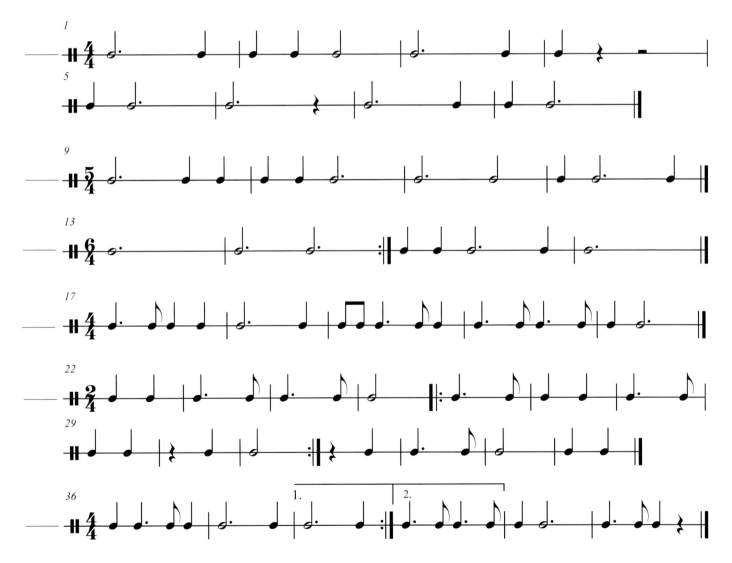

*1-10*

# Rhythm Sheet:
## 16th notes

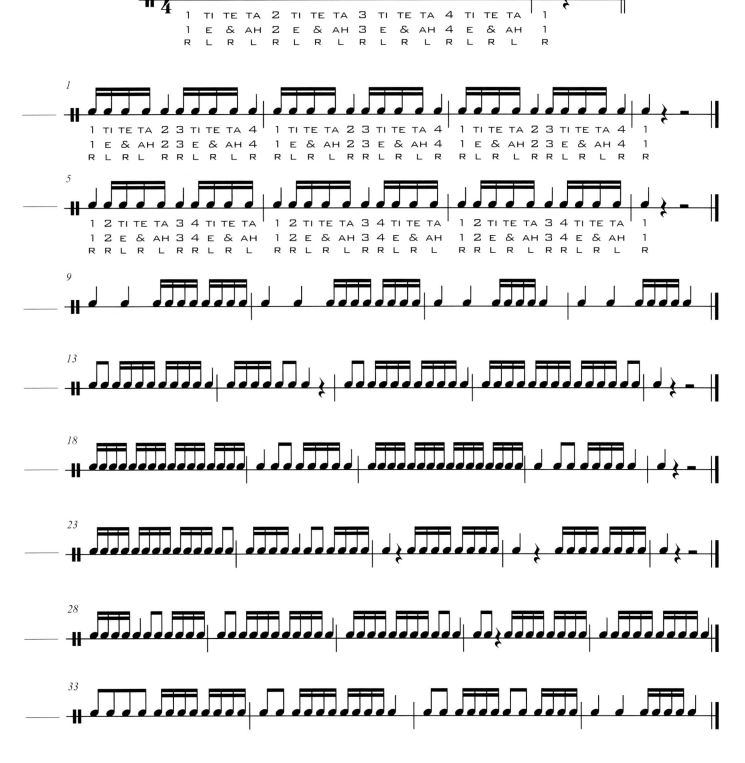

# Rhythm Sheet:
## More 16th Notes...

# RHYTHM SHEET:
## WAIT FOR IT #1

*1-13*

# RHYTHM SHEET:
## CHECKPOINT 1

PAY CLOSE ATTENTION TO THE DYNAMICS!!!

*1-14*

# Rhythm Sheet:
## 16th permutations

# RHYTHM SHEET:
## 1-TI-TE

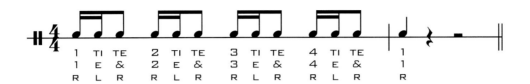

# Rhythm Sheet:
## 1-te-ta

*1-17*

# RHYTHM SHEET:
## TI-TE-TA

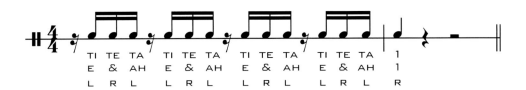

1-18

# RHYTHM SHEET:
## 1-TI-TA

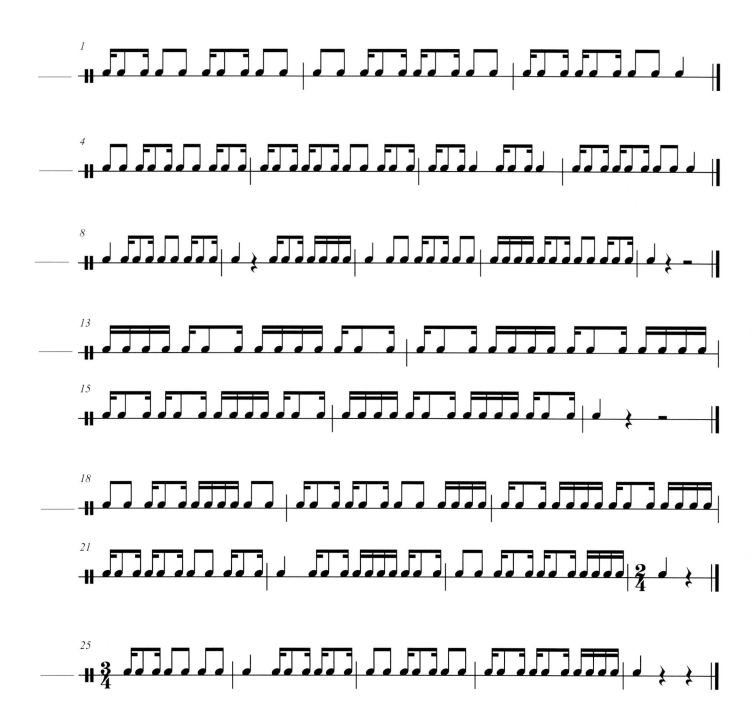

*1-19*

# Rhythm Sheet:
## 3 note permutations #1

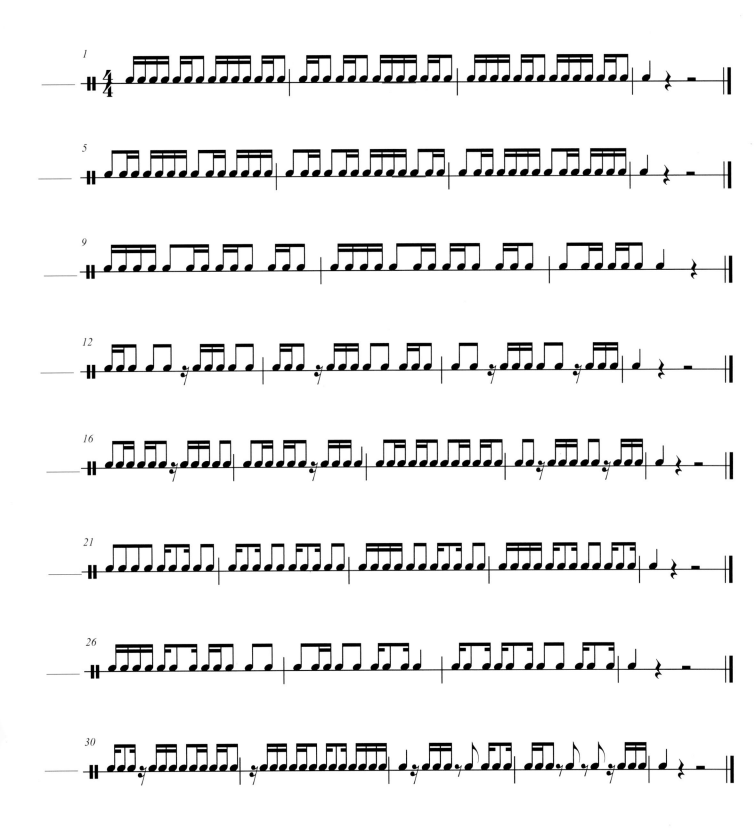

1-20

# RHYTHM SHEET:
## 3 NOTE PERMUTATIONS #2

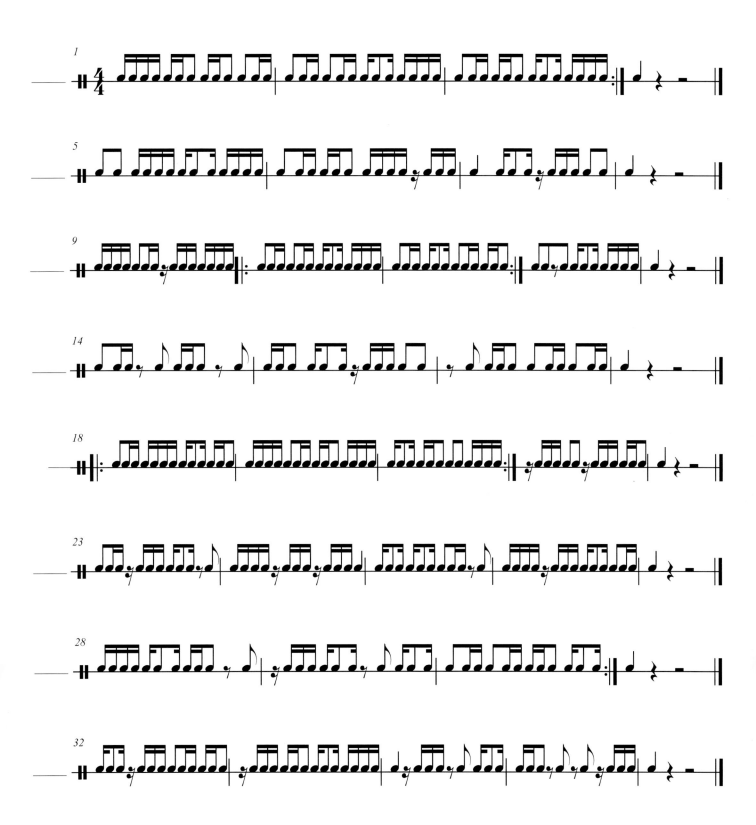

1-21

# RHYTHM SHEET:
## 3 NOTE PERMUTATIONS #3

*1-22*

# Rhythm Sheet:
## Wait For It #2

# RHYTHM SHEET:
## CHECKPOINT 2

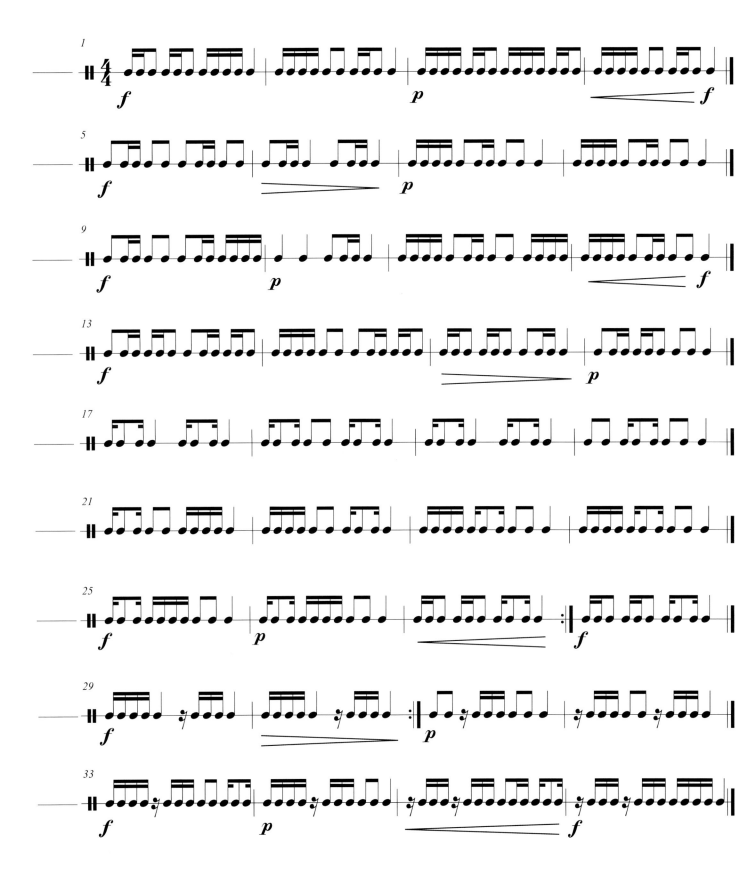

# RHYTHM SHEET:
## 1 - TI

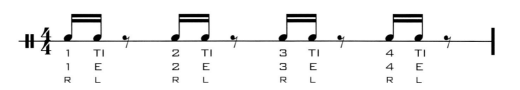

*1-25*

# RHYTHM SHEET:
## TE - TA

# RHYTHM SHEET:
## TI - TE

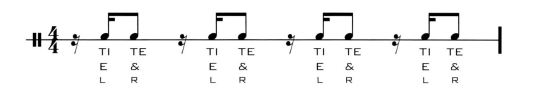

# Rhythm Sheet:
## 1 - TA

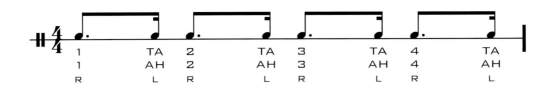

# Rhythm Sheet:
## 2 note permutations #1

# RHYTHM SHEET:
## 2 NOTE PERMUTATIONS #2

# RHYTHM SHEET:
## 2 NOTE PERMUTATIONS #3

1-31

# RHYTHM SHEET:
## WAIT FOR IT #3

# Rhythm Sheet:
## Checkpoint 3

*1-33*

# RHYTHM SHEET:
## TI

# Rhythm Sheet:
## TA

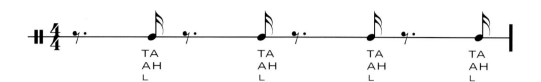

1-35

# Rhythm Sheet:
## 8th note triplets #1

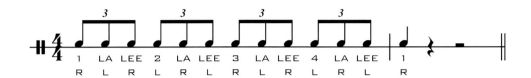

*1-36*

# Rhythm Sheet:
## 8th note triplets #2

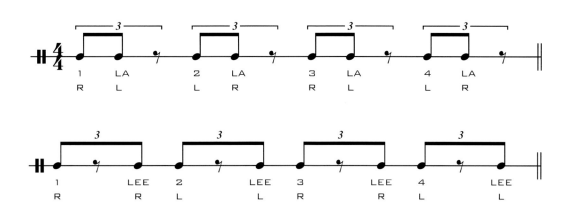

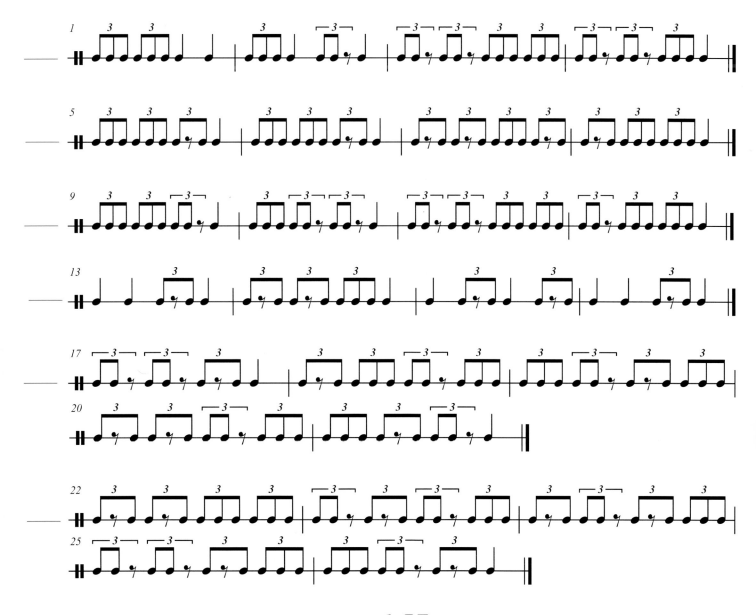

1-37

# Rhythm Sheet:
## 8th note triplets #3

1-38

# Rhythm Sheet:
## triplet permutations

1-39

# Rhythm Sheet:
## 16th note triplets

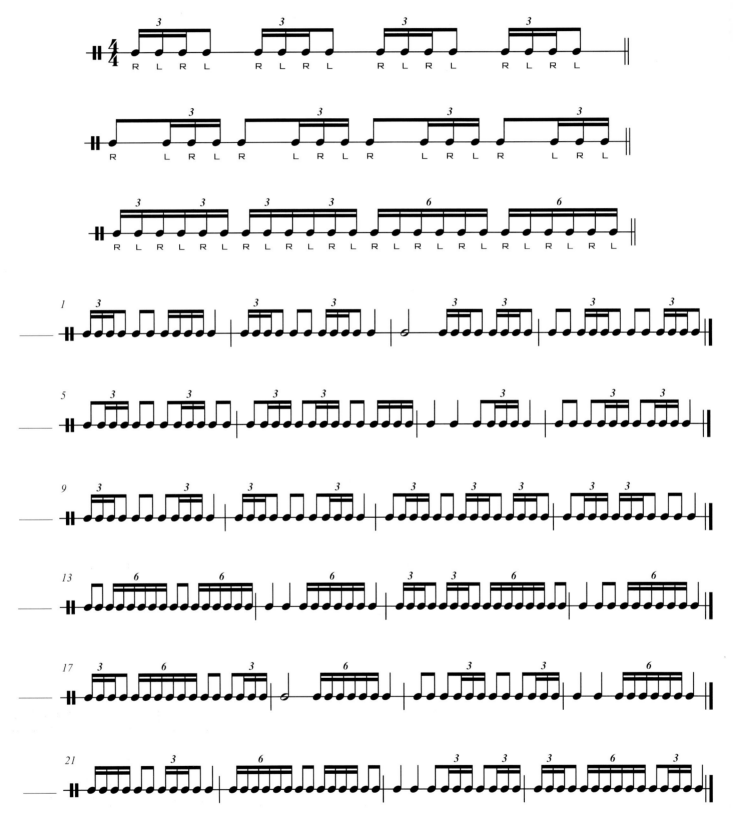

*1-40*

# RHYTHM SHEET:
## 12/8 TIME SIGNATURE

*ALL STICKINGS ARE "SUGGESTED PERFORMANCE STICKINGS" AND
DO NOT FOLLOW THE RH LEAD SYSTEM

*1-41*

# RHYTHM SHEET:
## 6/8 TIME SIGNATURE

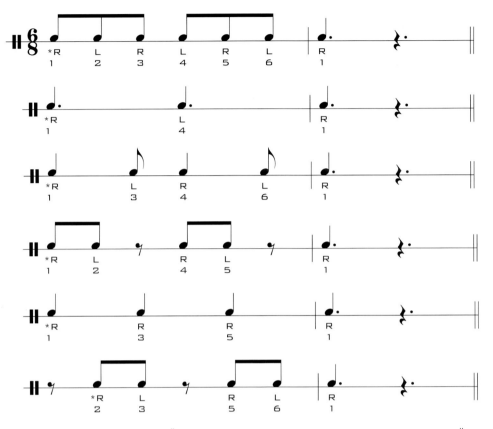

*ALL STICKINGS ARE "SUGGESTED PERFORMANCE STICKINGS" AND
DO NOT FOLLOW THE RH LEAD SYSTEM

*1-42*

# RHYTHM SHEET:
## 6/8 TIME SIGNATURE (W/16THS)

*1-43*

# Rhythm Sheet:
## 12/8, 6/8 & 3/8 Time Signatures

1-44

# Rhythm Sheet:
## 5 and 7

EXAMPLE 1:

-EACH RHYTHM MUST CORRECTLY FIT IN THE QUARTER NOTE SPACE.

-RH LEAD ALTERNATING IS NO LONGER THE STICKING SYSTEM USED. THE PRIORITY IS ON THE "CORRECT RHYTHM" AND NOT THE "CORRECT STICKING".

*CHECK PATTERN

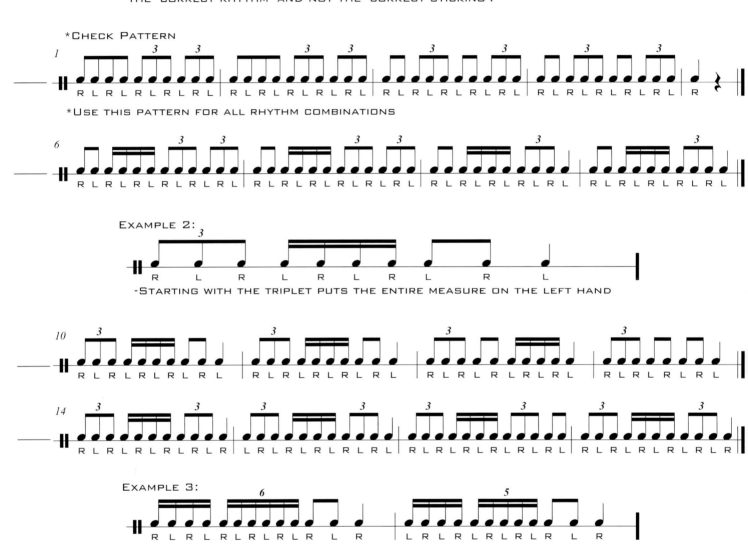

*USE THIS PATTERN FOR ALL RHYTHM COMBINATIONS

EXAMPLE 2:

-STARTING WITH THE TRIPLET PUTS THE ENTIRE MEASURE ON THE LEFT HAND

EXAMPLE 3:

-ADD 5'S, 6'S AND ANY OTHER TUPLET

-EACH RHYTHM MUST CORRECTLY FIT IN THE QUARTER NOTE SPACE

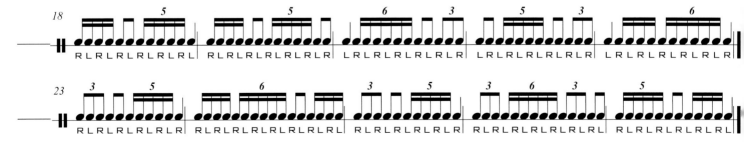

# Rhythm Sheet:
## Hand Speed Control - 2

# RHYTHM SHEET:
# HEMIOLAS

## HEMIOLA: LAYERING OF RHYTHMS BASED ON THE RATIO OF 3:2

NOT     VE - RY     HARD

### CAN BE LEARNED USING THE VOCAL: "NOT VERY HARD"

RIGHT HAND - 3

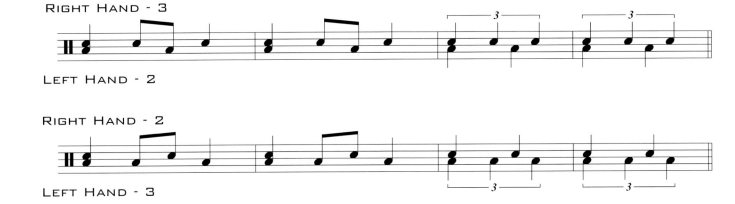

LEFT HAND - 2

RIGHT HAND - 2

LEFT HAND - 3

## ANOTHER COMMON "LAYERED" RHYTHM IS THE 3:4 RATIO

PASS     THE SALT AND     BUT-TER

### CAN BE LEARNED USING THE VOCAL: "PASS THE SALT AND BUTTER"

RIGHT HAND - 3

LEFT HAND - 4

RIGHT HAND - 4

LEFT HAND - 3

*1-48*

# SECTION TWO

# CHOPS

# CHOPS:
## STROKES CONTROL

THE FOLLOWING LINES OF TEXT REPRESENT THE RIGHT AND LEFT HANDS. THESE LINES ARE DESIGNED TO INTRODUCE THE CONCEPTS OF:

1. *LEGATO STROKES*: THE STROKE THAT USES REBOUND TO RETURN TO THE HEIGHT AT THE TOP OF ITS STICK PATH. (EXAMPLE: A 12" LEGATO STROKE WILL REBOUND AND END AT 12" FROM THE PLAYING SURFACE.)
LEGATO STROKES ARE USED ANY TIME THE SAME HEIGHT IS NEEDED IN CONSECUTIVE HITS.

2. *STACCATO STROKES*: THE STROKE THAT HAS NO REBOUND AND ENDS DOWN IN PLAYING POSITION (USUALLY ½" FROM THE PLAYING SURFACE.)
STACCATO STROKES ARE USED WHEN CHANGING FROM HIGHER TO LOWER HEIGHTS, FINISHING A NOTE BEFORE A REST, AND SWITCHING HANDS.

3. *RUDIMENTS:* THE STICKINGS USED IN CREATING SOME OF THE PARADIDDLE FAMILY AND ROLL FAMILY OF RUDIMENTS ARE PRESENT.

| | | | | |
|---|---|---|---|---|
| A. | R R R R | R R R R | R R R R | R R R R |
| B. | L L L L | L L L L | L L L L | L L L L |
| C. | R R R R | R R R R | L L L L | L L L L |
| D. | R R R R | L L L L | R R R R | L L L L |
| E. | R R L L | R R L L | R R L L | R R L L |
| F. | R L L R | R L L R | R L L R | R L L R |
| G. | R L R R | L R L L | R L R R | L R L L |
| H. | R R L R | L L R L | R R L R | L L R L |
| I. | R R L L | R L R R | L L R R | L R L L |
| J. | R L R R | L L R R | L R L L | R R L L |

2-1

# Chops:
## No Stone Unturned

## REMOVE RESTS TO CREATE MORE VARIATIONS

*2-2*

# Chops:
# Legatos #1

**16 On a Hand w/ Variations**

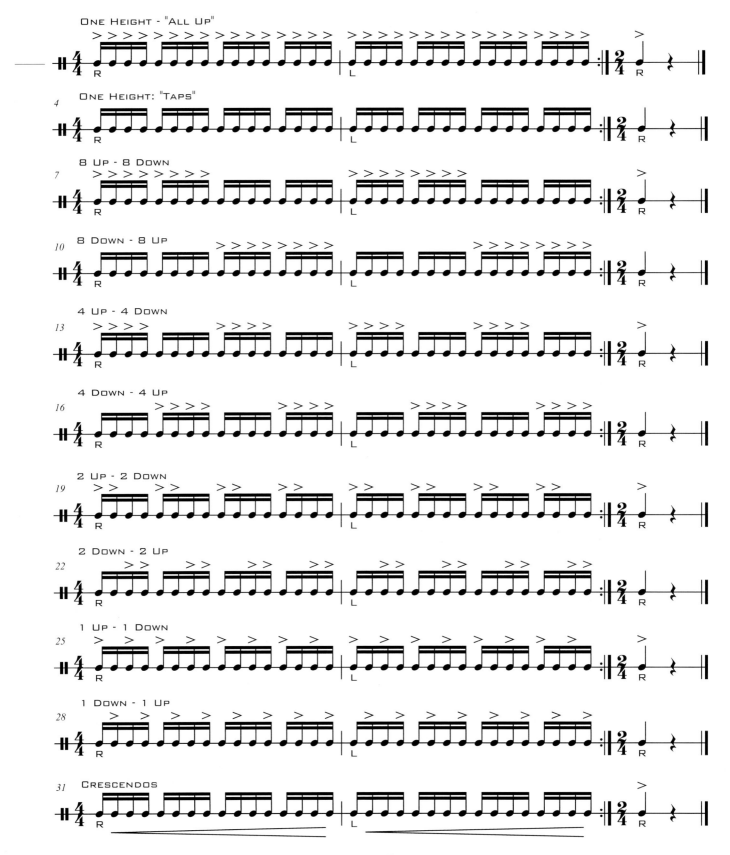

# CHOPS:
# LEGATOS #2

**COUNTDOWN W/ VARIATIONS**

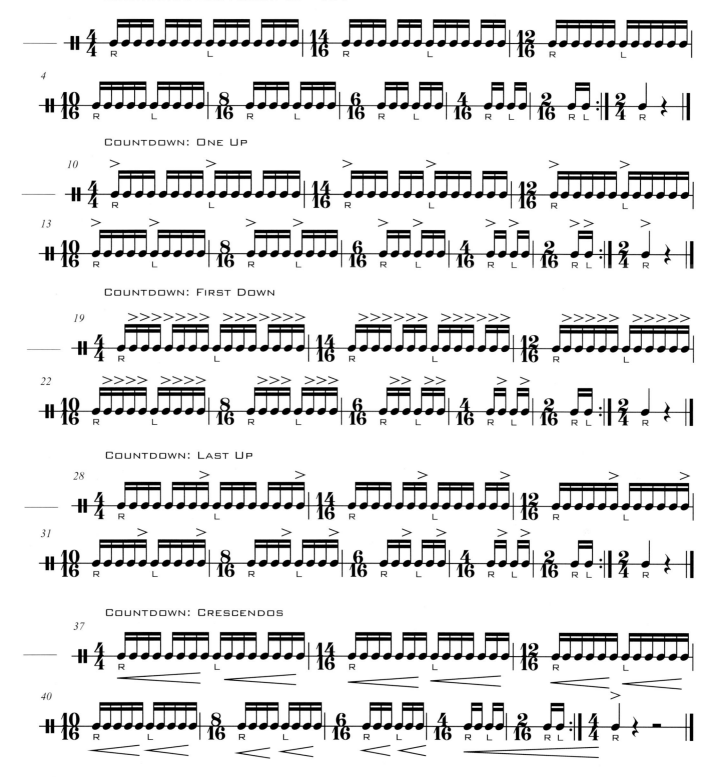

# Chops:
# Legatos #3

# Chops:
# Legatos: Hand to Hand #1

# Chops:

## Stick Control - 16th Notes

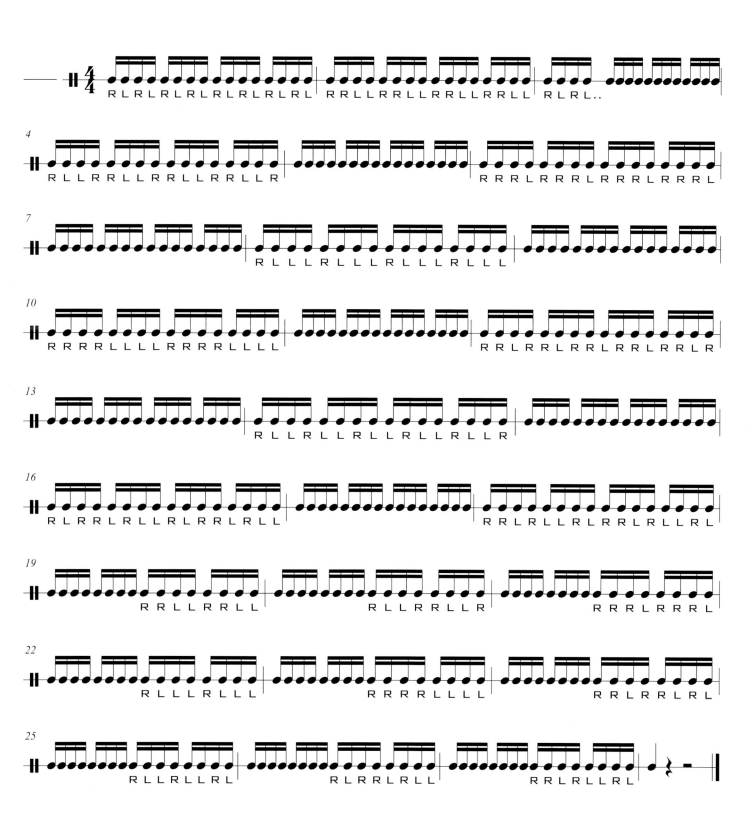

# CHOPS:

## STICK CONTROL - TRIPLETS

# Chops:
## puh-duh-das #1

> Lines should be played as one height and THEN add the accents to create the two height variations...

2-10

# Chops:
## puh-duh-das #2

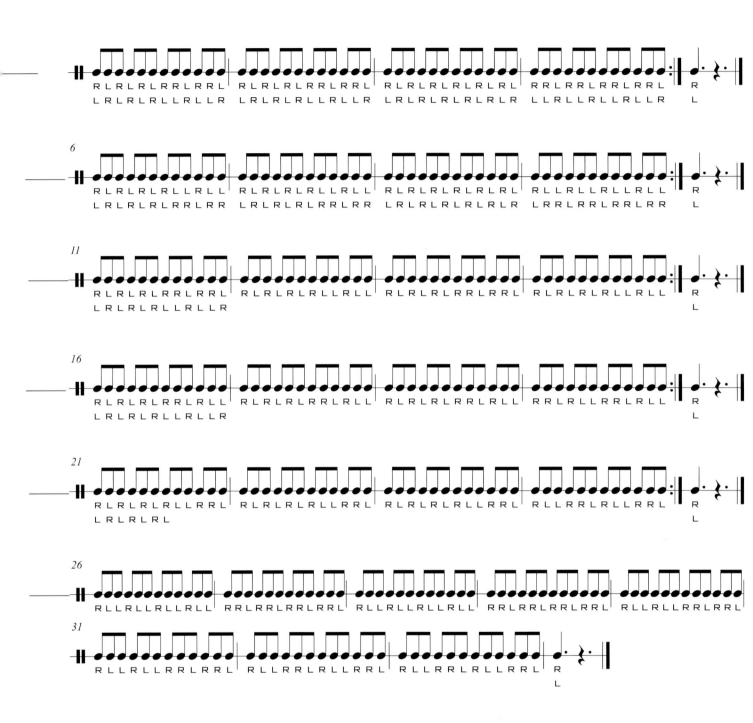

**\*Add accents to create 2-height variations\***

# CHOPS:
## UNLEAD YOURSELF

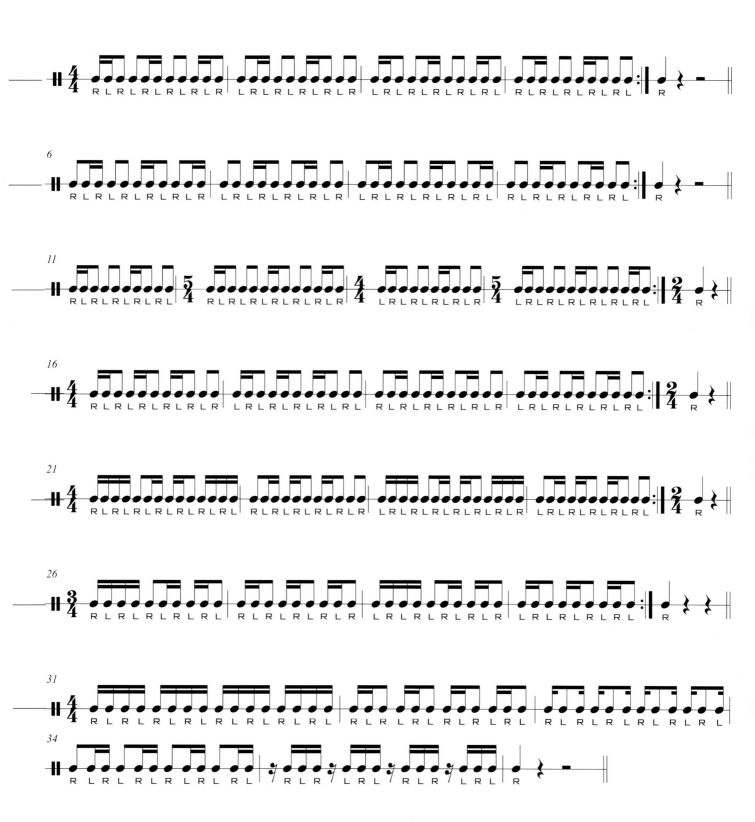

# Chops:
## Tap/Accent #1

# Chops:
# Tap/Accent #2

# Chops:
## Alternating T/A #1

# Chops:
## Alternating T/A #2

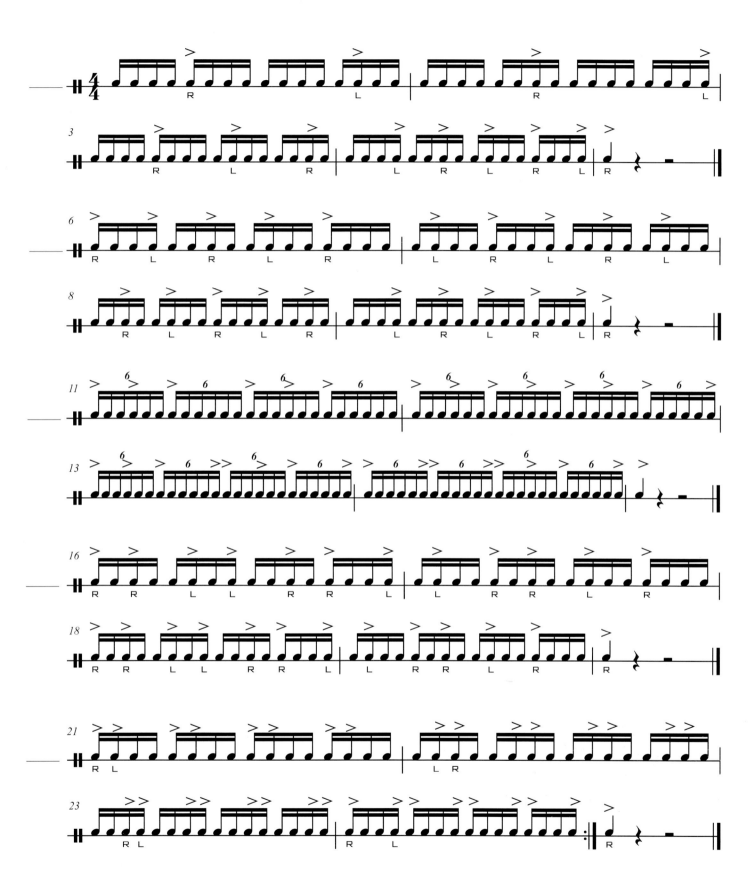

# CHOPS:
## THE GRID - 16TH NOTES

### THE GRID:

A PERMUTATION-BASED DRUMMING CONCEPT THAT USES STATIONARY VS. MOVING VARIABLES. THE MOST COMMONLY USED VARIABLES ARE ACCENTS, FLAMS, AND DIDDLES. BY COMBINING THESE VARIABLES AS EITHER STATIONARY OR MOVING, A WHOLE WORLD OF COOL RUDIMENTAL PATTERNS CAN BE DISCOVERED. THE MORE PERMUTATIONS THAT YOU LEARN AND MASTER, THE MORE SOPHISTICATED YOUR DRUMMING VOCABULARY.

IF YOU WANT TO TAKE YOUR RUDIMENTAL DRUMMING SKILLS TO AN ADVANCED LEVEL, IT IS IMPERATIVE THAT YOU LEARN *THE GRID*.

### *PLUS, IT'S FUN!!!!*

-------------------------------------------------------------------------------------

> THE GRID IS COMMONLY PLAYED WITH A 4 - 2 - 1 SEQUENCE. THIS MEANS THAT THE CHOSEN PERMUTATIONS ARE PLAYED :

- FOUR TIMES EACH / ONE TIME THROUGH
- TWO TIMES EACH / TWO TIMES THROUGH
- ONE TIME EACH / FOUR TIMES THROUGH.

4 - 2 - 1 PATTERN SEQUENCE: SINGLE ACCENT GRID

> IN THE ABOVE GRID, THE *MOVING VARIABLE* IS A SINGLE ACCENT. THIS MEANS THAT THE ACCENT MOVES THROUGH THE FOUR 16TH NOTES IN THE RHYTHM. A NEW PERMUTATION IS FORMED EACH TIME THAT HAPPENS.
> NOW TRY IT AS A DOUBLE ACCENT GRID...

16TH NOTE DOUBLE ACCENT GRID

*2-17*

# CHOPS:
## THE GRID - 16TH NOTES

> THE NEXT GRID IS AN EXAMPLE OF A *MOVING VARIABLE* AND A *STATIONARY VARIABLE*. TO MAKE THIS GRID WE WILL USE THE SINGLE ACCENT AS THE *MOVING VARIABLE* AND THE DRAG (DIDDLE) ON THE SECOND 16TH NOTE AS THE *STATIONARY VARIABLE*.

16TH NOTE SINGLE ACCENT W/ DRAG

> THIS GRID IS THE OPPOSITE OF THE ABOVE GRID: THE DIDDLE IS NOW THE *MOVING VARIABLE* WHILE THE SINGLE ACCENT IS THE *STATIONARY VARIABLE*.

16 NOTE DIDDLE WITH SINGLE ACCENT

> DON'T FORGET THAT ALL GRIDS SHOULD BE STARTED ON THE RIGHT AND LEFT HANDS. <

# Chops:
## The Grid - 16th Notes

> Another option for playing the grid is to play the sequence backwards. By starting the accent on the fourth 16th and then proceeding to the third, second and first.

16 Note single accent - backwards

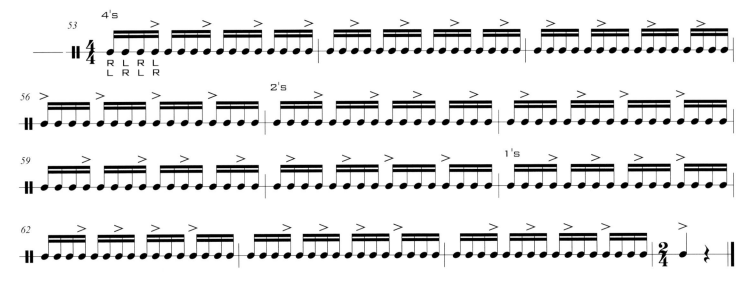

16 Note double accent - backwards

> More grid options:

- change the order of the 4-2-1 pattern to create new sequences:
    - 1-2-4    - 2-1-4    - 2-4-1    - 4-1-2    - 1-4-2

- Use flams, accents and diddles to create as many grids as possible. the more you learn, the better a player you become...

# Chops:
## The Grid - Triplets

> The Grid can also be played with triplets as the skeleton rhythm. The triplet grid is very common in the highest levels of the modern rudimental vocabulary. Some of the benefits of working the triplet grid are:

- constant alternating of hands
- patterns that move "over the barline"
- mastering rudiments that prepare you for higher levels of literature

**Triplet single accent grid**

> Next Grid:
> *Stationary Variable:* Drag / *Moving Variable:* Single Accent

**Triplet Tap Drag Grid**

*2-20*

# Chops:
# The Grid - Triplets

> The most important triplet grid is the flam accent. In order to move into the higher level rudimental literature, you must learn the flam accent grid. *It is essential to learn this grid at a slow tempo to ensure it is performed correctly.*

Flam Accent Grid

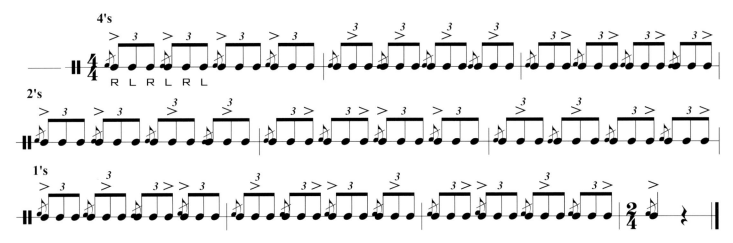

Flam Drag Grid

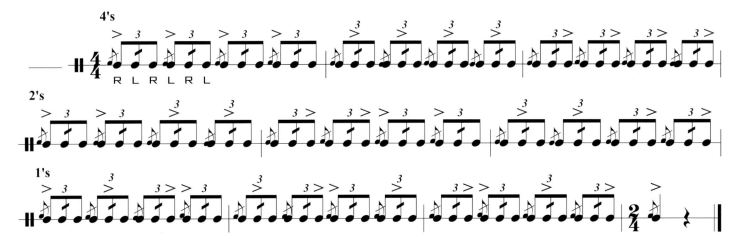

> Remember that any grid can be changed by switching the *Stationary* and *Moving Variables*.
   - Flam Accent Grid:
        *Stationary: Accent / Moving: Flam*
   - Flam Drag Grid:
        *Stationary: accent / Moving: Flam Drag*
   - Etc...

*2-21*

# Chops:
## The Grid - Triplets

> The next two grids are also important for developing an advanced vocabulary. They are the natural progressions built from the Flam Accent and Flam Drag Grids.

> Try it with a second flam added. Be creative on which two counts you place them.

> Also: add diddles as well!!!

# Chops:
# Doubles #1

# Chops:
# Doubles #2

# Chops:
# Double Beat 2011

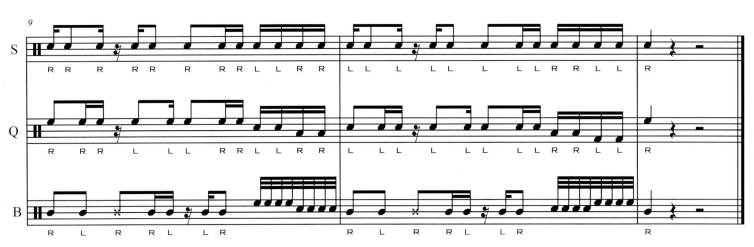

*2-25*

# Chops:
## Double Beat 2014

# Chops:
## Criddles - Diddles #1

# Chops:
## Criddles w/ 16th skeleton

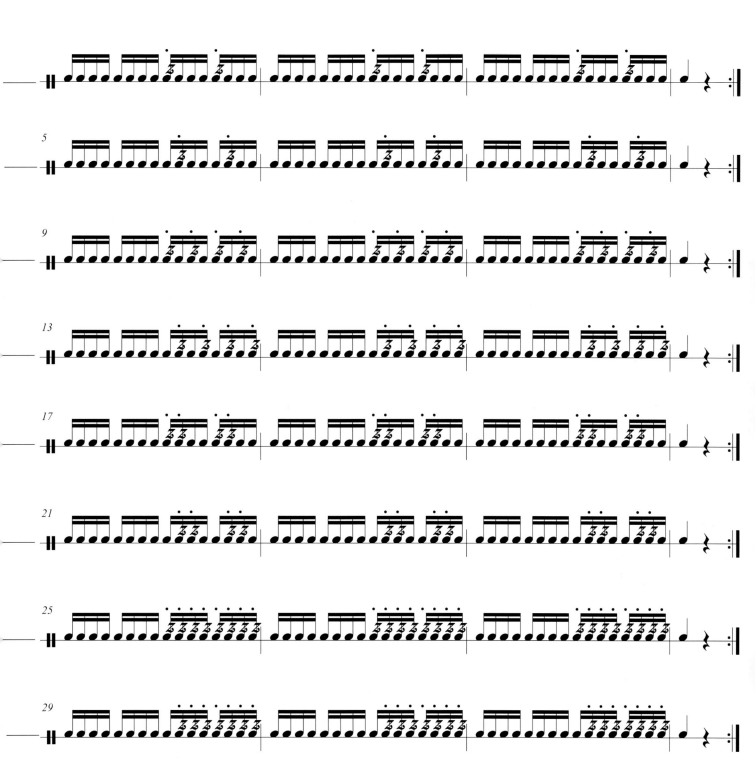

# Chops:
## Diddles w/ 16th skeleton

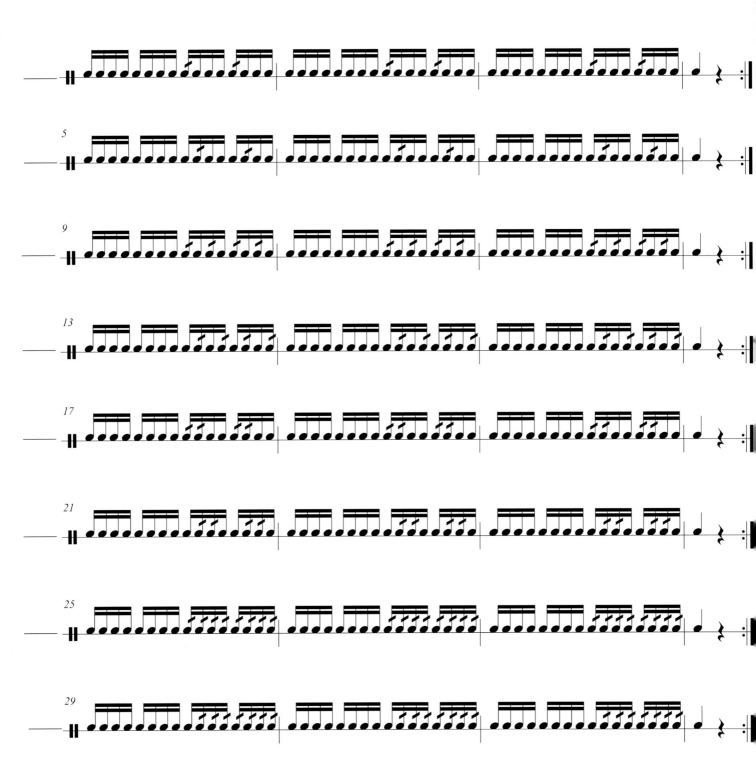

*2-29*

# Chops:
## Criddles - Diddles #2

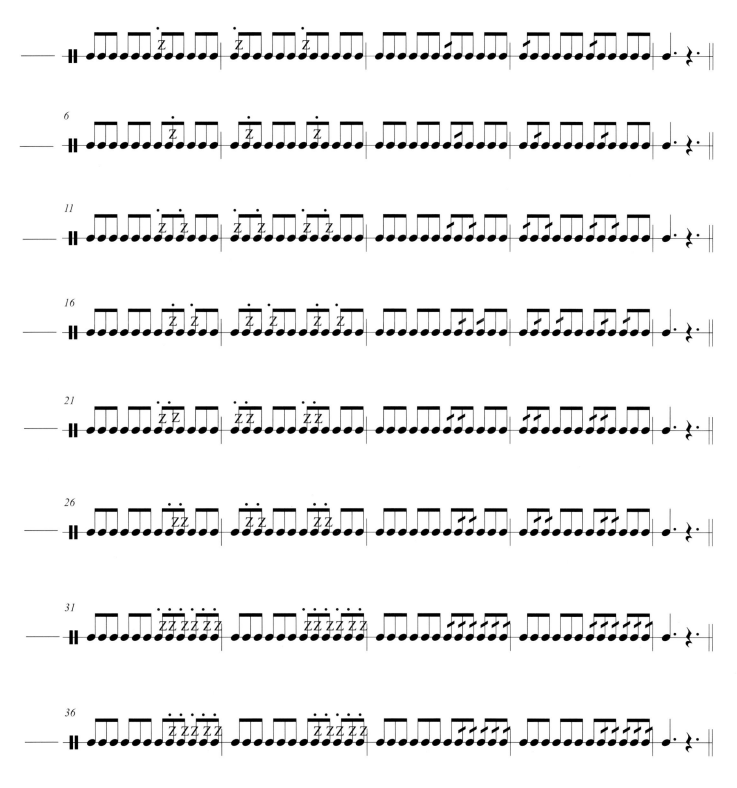

**\*ADD ACCENTS TO CREATE VARIATIONS\***

*2-30*

# CHOPS:
## CRIDDLES - DIDDLES #3

# Chops:
## Diddles w/ triplet skeleton

*2-32*

# Chops:
## 3/4 Galop

VARIATIONS:
-ALL ONE HEIGHT
-ADD ACCENTS (ALL ELSE @ 3")

*2-33*

# SECTION THREE

# RUDIMENTS

# BASIC RUDIMENTS
## THE ONES YOU MUST KNOW...

### PARADIDDLES

### ROLLS

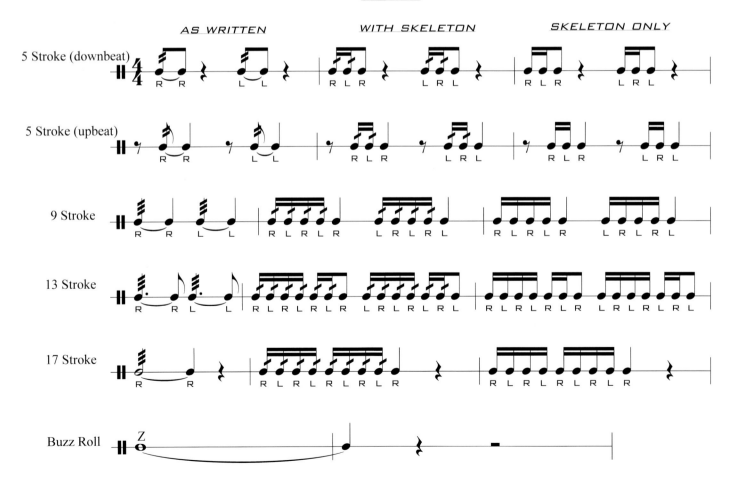

*3-1*

## FLAMS

## MISC.

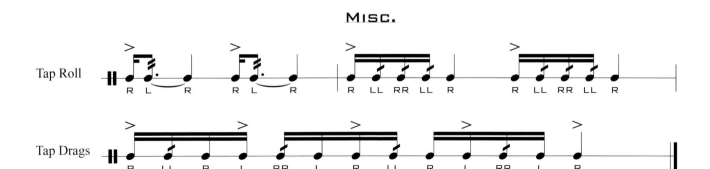

# RUDIMENTS:
## 5 ESSENTIAL STROKES

### (ANY 1-HANDED EXERCISE CAN BE PLAYED AS DOUBLE STOPS)

# RUDIMENTS:
## 5 Essential Strokes (cont.)

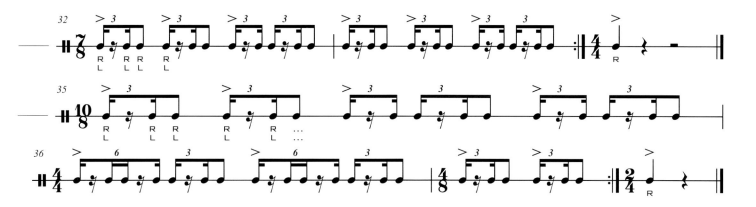

### 4. Hug-a-dit: flam taps, 3's, egg beaters, puhdadas, etc.

*All hug-a-dit strokes have a natural heights decay*

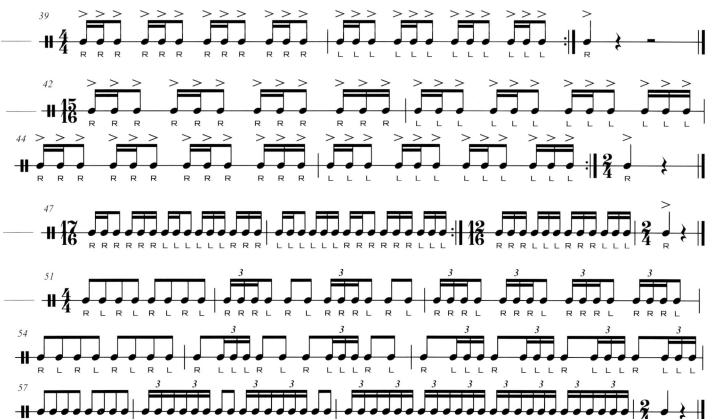

### 5. Upstroke: tap accent grids, inverts, chutadas, etc.

3" taps/ 15" accents

*3-4*

# RUDIMENTS:
## 5 Essential Strokes (cont.)

# Rudiments:
## Paradiddles #1

# Rudiments:
## Paradiddles #2

### Double Paradiddle

### Triple Paradiddle

# RUDIMENTS:
## PARADIDDLES #3

### PARADIDDLE-DIDDLE

# Rudiments:
## Paradiddles #4

# Rudiments:
## rolls - 15 patterns

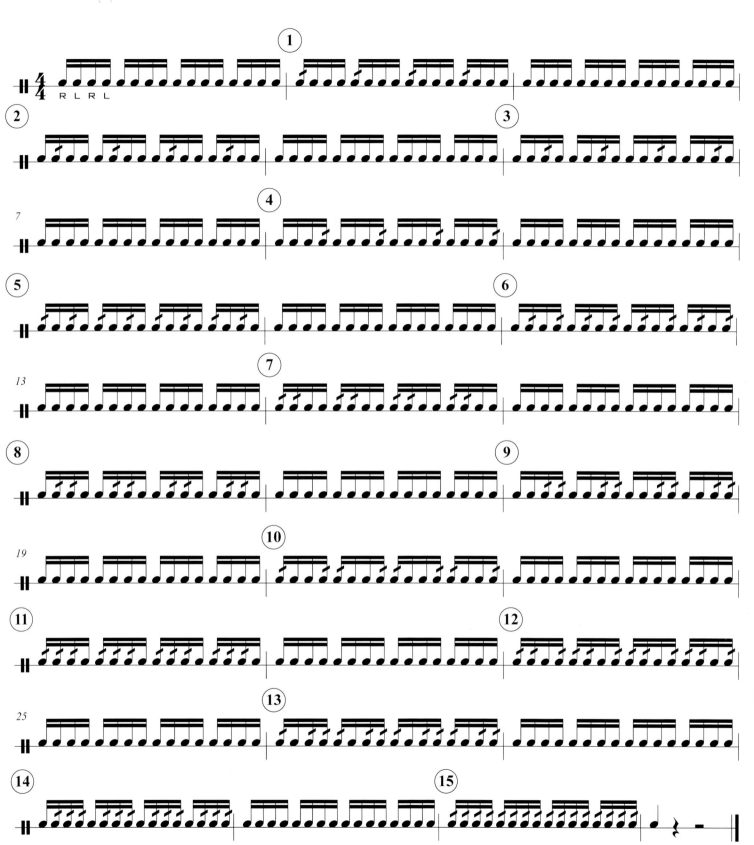

# RUDIMENTS:
## COMMON ROLLS INVENTORY

**AS WRITTEN**          **SKELETON**

# Rudiments:
## Rolls - 5 stroke

3-12

# RUDIMENTS:
## ROLLS - 9 STROKE

# Rudiments:
## rolls - 7, 13, and tap

# Rudiments:
## Tap Drags and Tap Fives

**Tap Drags**

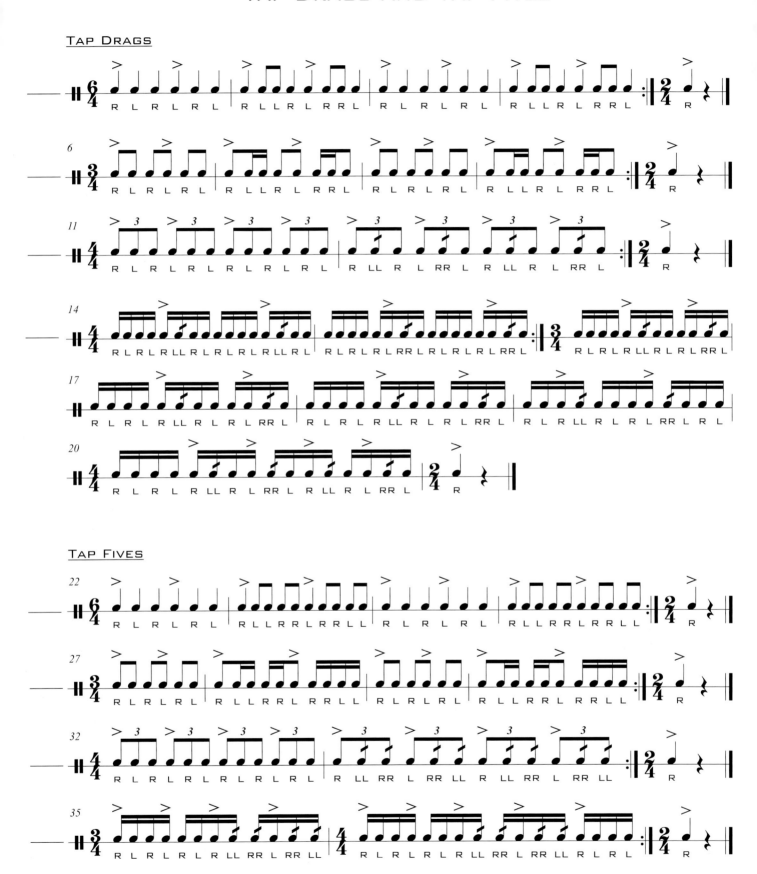

**Tap Fives**

*3-15*

# RUDIMENTS:
## TRIPLET ROLLS #1

# RUDIMENTS:
## TRIPLET ROLLS #2

3-17

# RUDIMENTS:
## CRIDDLES '14

*3-18*

# Rudiments:
## Isolated Flams

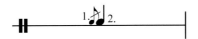

## Two Parts:

1. **Grace Note**: -usually 1" for isolated flams
   -controls the sound of the flam(open vs. closed)
   -*never lifted!!!!*

2. **Primary Stroke**: -determines name of flam (right or left)
   -the skeleton of the flam (rhythm with no grace note)
   -determines the volume (height) of the flam

# Rudiments:
# Flam Taps

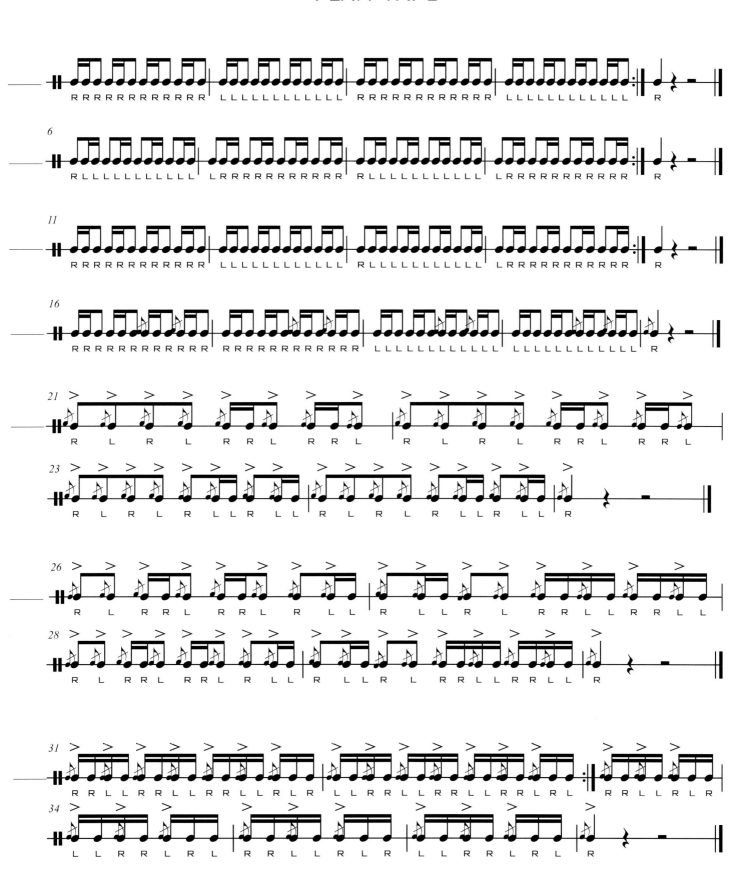

# RUDIMENTS:
## FLAM ACCENTS

# Rudiments:
## Flam paradiddles/ pataflaflas

### Flam Paradiddle

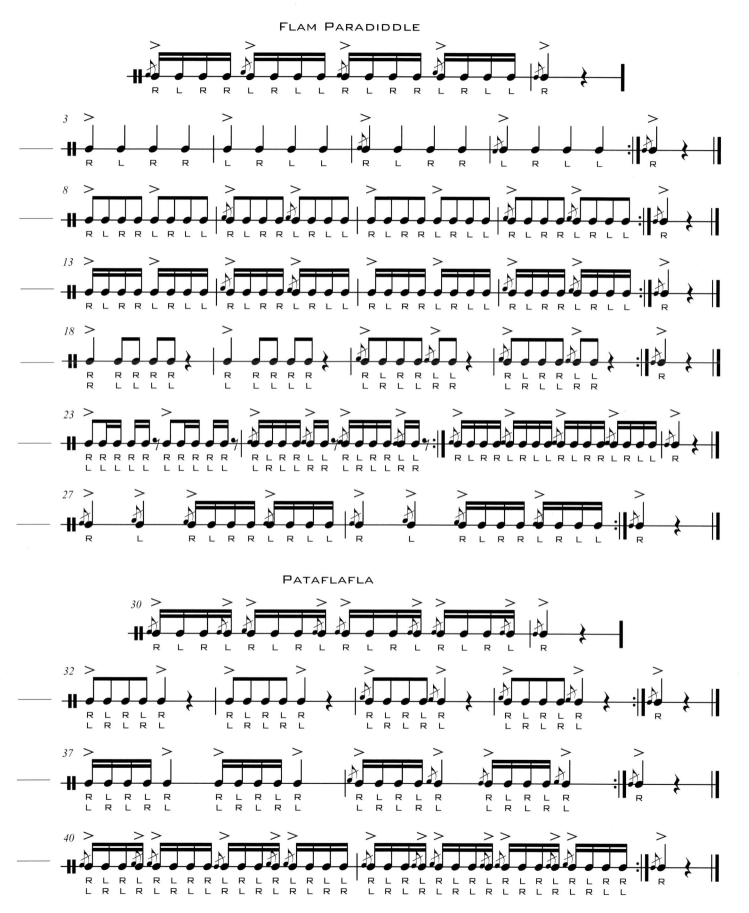

3-22

# RUDIMENTS:
## FLAMS - ADVANCED #1

**FLAM DRAGS**

**FLAM CHEESE**

3-23

# Rudiments:
## Flams - Advanced #2

### Flam Fives

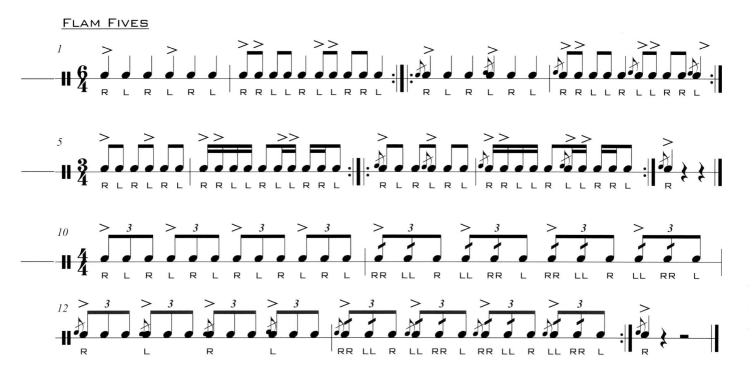

### A Shopping Spree

### The Tag

*3-24*

# RUDIMENTS:
## FLAMS - ADVANCED #3

# Rudiments:
# Flams - Advanced #4

**Upstroke Chugadas**

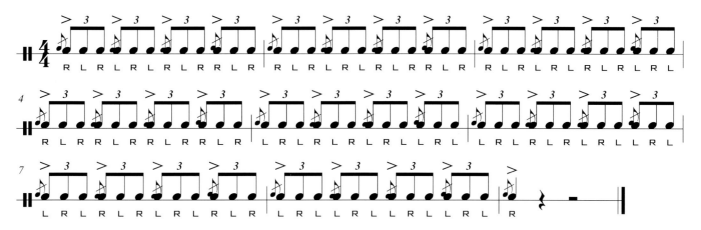

Variations:
- Add Flam Drags
- Add Cheeses
- Add Flam Fives
- Add Chutachas
- Add Cheese Chutachas
- Create your own...

**Downstroke Chugadas**

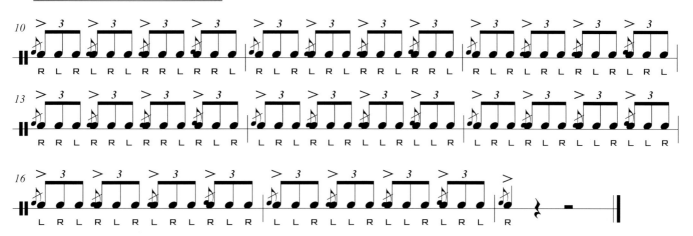

Variations:
- Add Flam Drags
- Add Cheeses
- Add Flam Fives
- Add Chutachas
- Add Cheese Chutachas
- Create your own...

*3-26*

# Rudiments:
## Odd Meter Flams

**Skeleton**

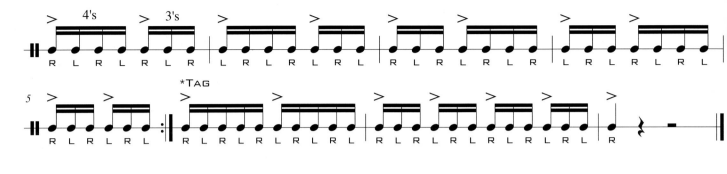

**Flams**

**Tap Drags**

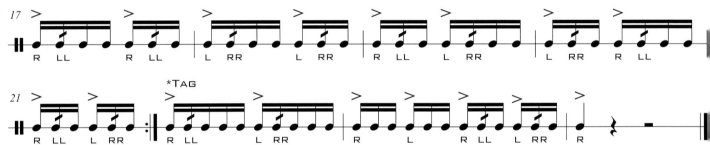

## Variations:

-On the 4's:
   Rolls, Tap Rolls, Paradiddles, paradiddle-diddles, 3's, Flam Taps
Inverts, Pataflaflas

-On the 3's:
   Flam Drags, Cheeses, Flam Fives, Chuta-chas, Ta-Chutas,

*See Tag Variations Page

*3-27*

# Rudiments:
## Odd Meter Flams - Tag Variations

# RUDIMENTS:
## CHICAGO 4

*ADD FLAMS FOR HARDER VARIATIONS

3-29

# Rudiments:
## Advanced Rudiments list

BOOK REPORT

DOUBLE FLAM DRAG

TA-CHUTA

TA-CHEESE-TA

CHUTA-CHA

INVERT CHUTA-CHA

CHEESE CHUTA-CHA

INVERT CHEESE CHUTA-CHA

FLAM FIVE FLAFLA

SAME HAND FLAM FIVE FLAFLA

EGG BEATERS

THREE'S (FRENCH ROLL)

HERTA

3-31

©FECIV

# SECTION FOUR

# MALLETS

# Mallets:
## Note Naming

The first pages of the Mallets Section are dedicated to the development of note naming speed and accuracy. There are many ways to utilize these exercises and here are a few suggestions:

-<u>Say the note names out loud as quickly as possible</u> while focusing on accuracy and clear articulation of the note name.

-<u>Write the names of the notes under each one</u> while working as fast as possible with 100% accuracy. *(Remember to use capital letters for each note name.)*

-<u>Say each note name out loud while touching the correct bar on the keyboard instrument.</u> This will develop spatial awareness of the instrument as well as the peripheral reading technique.

-<u>Play each note on the keyboard while saying its name out loud.</u> This will develop the aural recognition of the note while still strengthening the spatial awareness of the instrument and peripheral reading technique.

***REMEMBER TO ALWAYS KEEP YOUR EYES ON THE MUSIC***

# Mallets:
## Note Naming #1

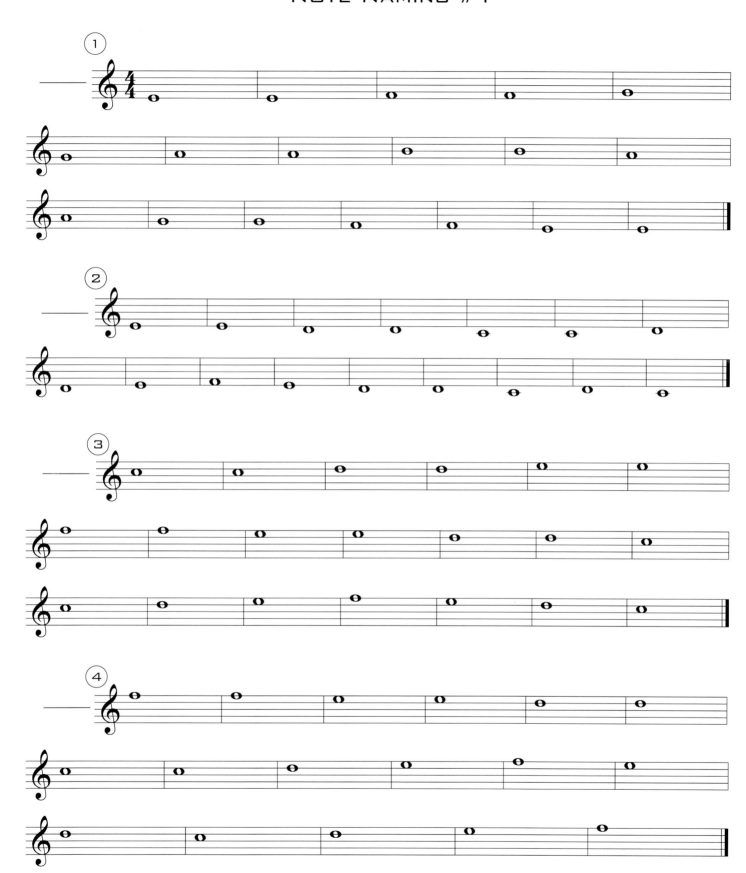

# MALLETS:
## NOTE NAMING #2

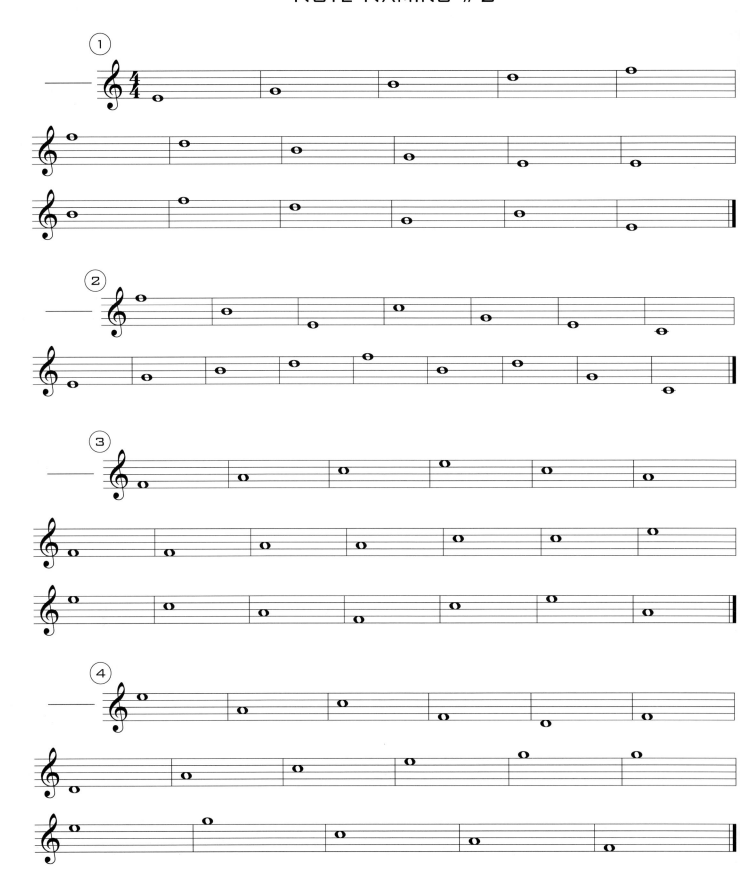

4-2

# Mallets:
## Note Naming #3

*4-3*

# Mallets:
## Note Naming #4

4-4

# Mallets:
## Note Naming #5

# Mallets:
## Note Naming #6

4-6

# Mallets:
# Reading Process

- This reading process is to be used with the mallet reading pages 4-9 to 4-14.

- The notes in this section are not written in any set time signatures, key signatures or rhythms. These items are meant to decided and changed each time a section or line is practiced.

- a metronome is essential to keep the notes (and performer) moving in time.

- *The most important rule is to always keep your eyes on the music, not the keyboard!!!*

### Reading process

1. With hands in pockets, say the name of the pitches
2. Touch the keyboard and say the names of the pitches
3. Air drum and say the name of the pitches
4. Play and say the names of the pitches

The pitches are read with following rhythms:

1. whole notes (as written)
2. half notes
3. quarter notes
4. eighth notes

# Mallets:
# reading process - 2

Apply the following rhythms to the
note reading pages: 4-9 to 4-14.

*4-8*

# Mallets:
# Note Reading - 1

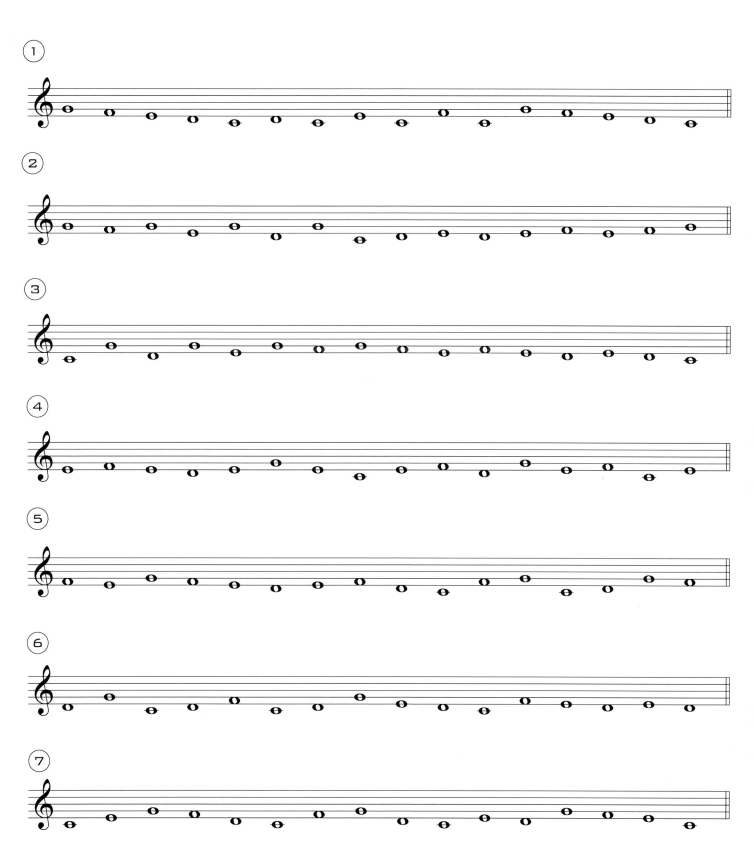

*4-9*

# Mallets:
# Note Reading - 2

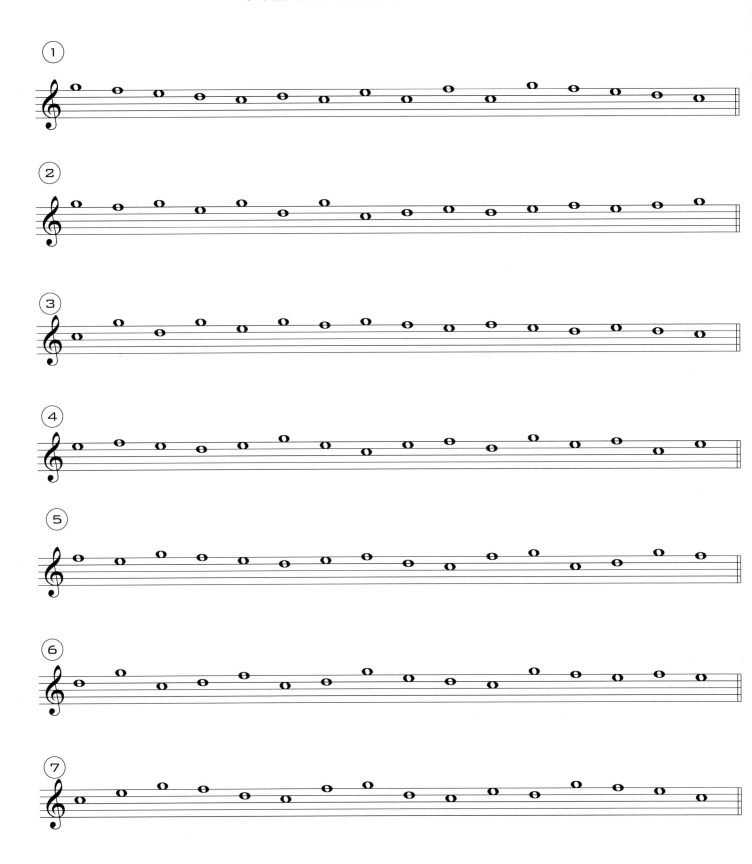

*4-10*

# Mallets:
# Note Reading - 3

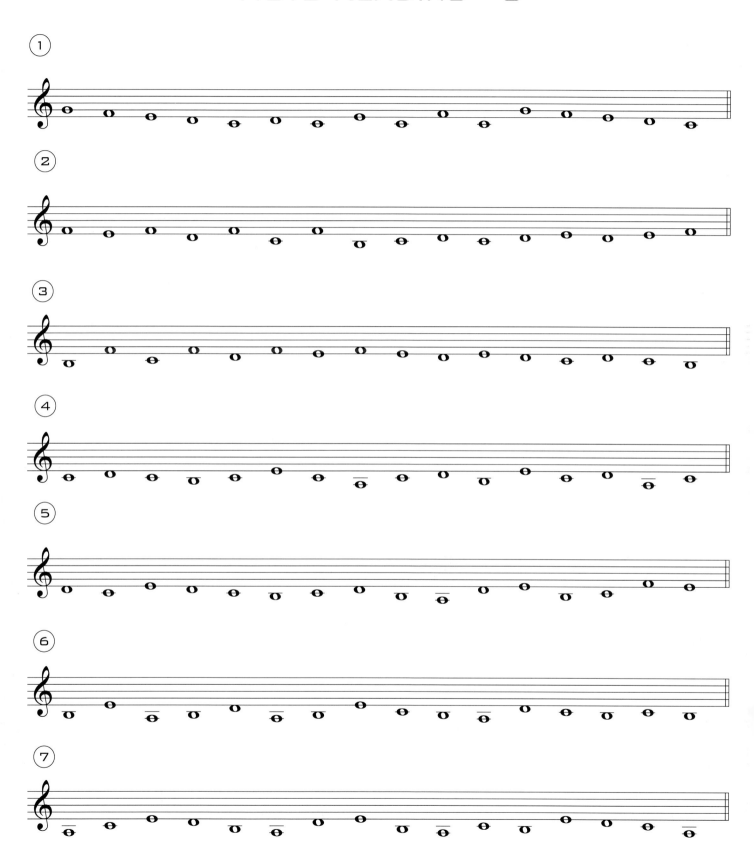

# Mallets:
# Note Reading - 4

# Mallets:
# Note Reading - 5

# Mallets:
# Note Reading - 6

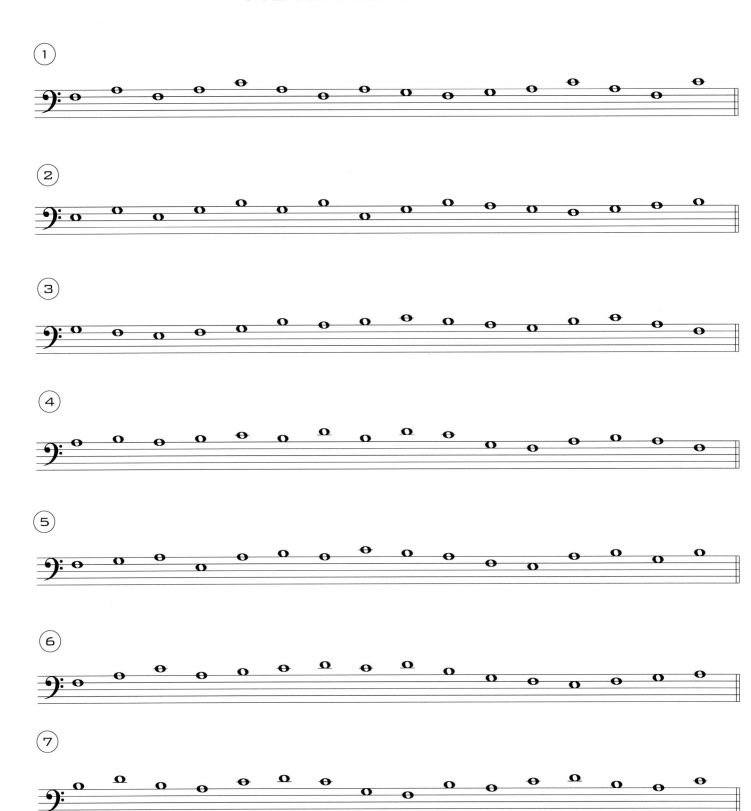

# Mallets:
## Major Scales - The Flats

- Perform all scales with pure alternating sticking: R - L - R - L - etc.

- Perform each scale starting on RH or LH

*4-15*

# Mallets:
## Scale Etudes #1

4-16

# Mallets:
## Scale Etudes #2

**F Scale**

**B-Flat Scale**

# Mallets:
## Scale Etudes #3

E-Flat Scale

A-Flat Scale

*4-18*

# Mallets:
## Major Scales - The Sharps

- Perform all scales with pure alternating sticking: R - L - R - L - etc.

- Perform each scale starting on RH or LH

*4-19*

# Mallets:
## Scale Etudes #4

G Scale

D Scale

*4-20*

# Mallets:
## Scale Etudes #5

**D Scale**

**A Scale**

*4-21*

# Mallets:
## Musical Etudes #1

**Hot Cross Buns**

English Folk Song

**Mary Had A Little Lamb**

**Au Claire De La Lune**

French Folk Song

**Twinkle, Twinkle Little Star**

Traditional

*4-22*

# Mallets:
## Musical Etudes #2

**Go Tell Aunt Rhodie**

American Folk Song

**London Bridge**

English Folk Song

**Yankee Doodle**

American Folk Song

**Lightly Row**

Traditional

*4-23*

# Mallets:
## Musical Etudes #3

JINGLE BELLS

J.L. PIERPONT

JOLLY OLD ST. NICK

J.L. PIERPONT

GOOD KING WENSCLESAS

T. HELMORE

*4-24*

# Mallets:
## Musical Etudes #4

Up On The Housetop

Traditional

Deck The Halls

Traditional

Auld Lang Sine

Scottish Folk Song

# Mallets:
## Musical Etudes #5

Ode To Joy — Beethoven

Minuet in G — J.S. Bach

Camptown Races — Stephen Foster

*4-26*

# Mallets:
## Musical Etudes #6

WHEN THE SAINTS GO MARCHING IN

TRADITIONAL

ORPHEUS IN THE UNDERWORLD

OFFENBACH

WILLIAM TELL OVERTURE

ROSSINI

*4-27*

# Mallets:
## Musical Etudes #7

**Hunter's Chorus**

von Weber

**On Top of Old Smokey**

American Folk Song

**Scarborough Fair**

English Folk Song

*4-28*

# Mallets:

## Natural Minor Scales - The Flats

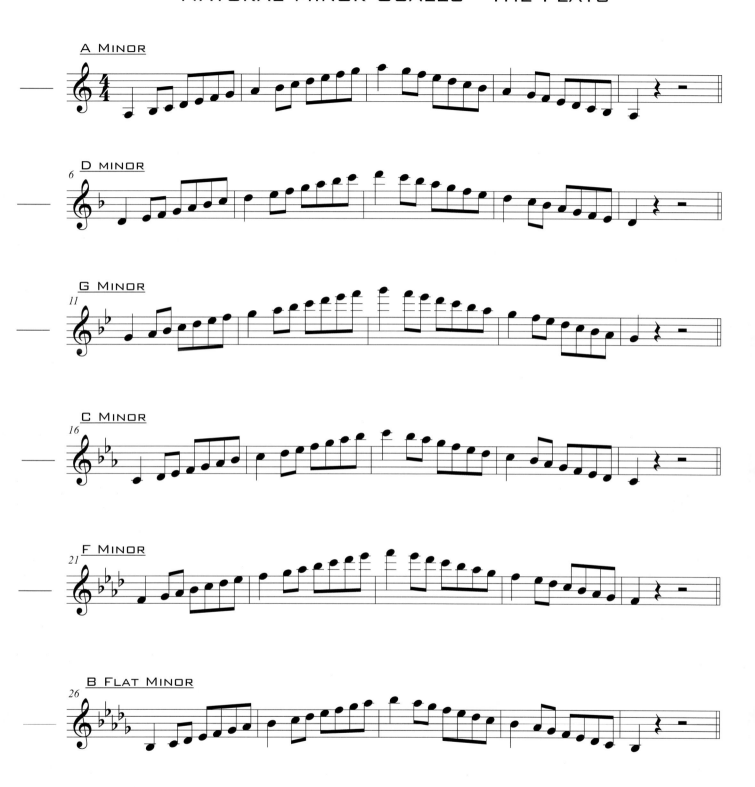

- Perform all scales with pure alternating sticking: R - L - R - L - etc.

- Perform each scale starting on RH or LH

*4-29*

# Mallets:

## Natural Minor Scales - The Sharps

A Minor

E Minor

B Minor

F# Minor

C# Minor

G# Minor

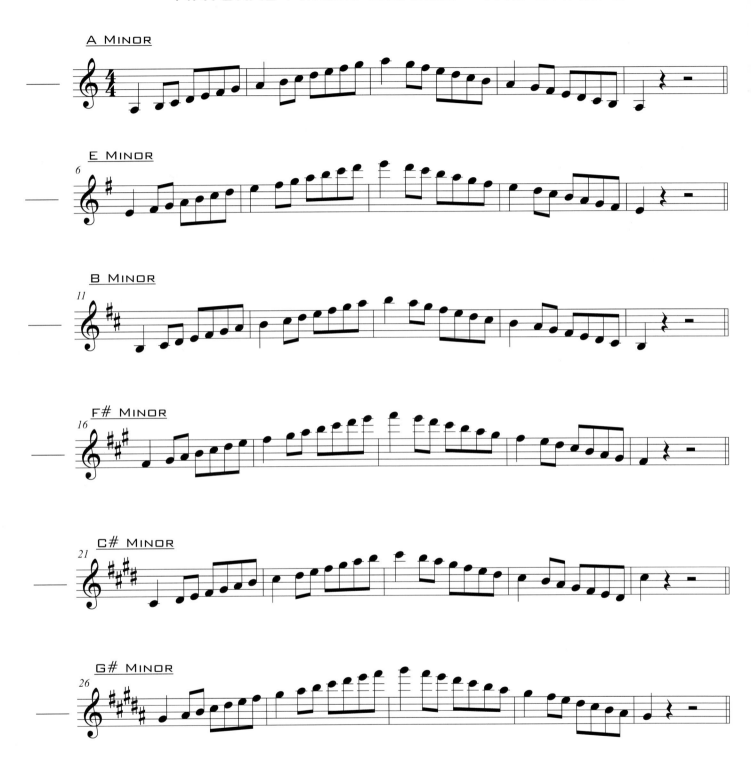

- Perform all scales with pure alternating sticking: R - L - R - L - etc.

- Perform each scale starting on RH or LH

*4-30*

# Mallets:
# Green Scales

C Major

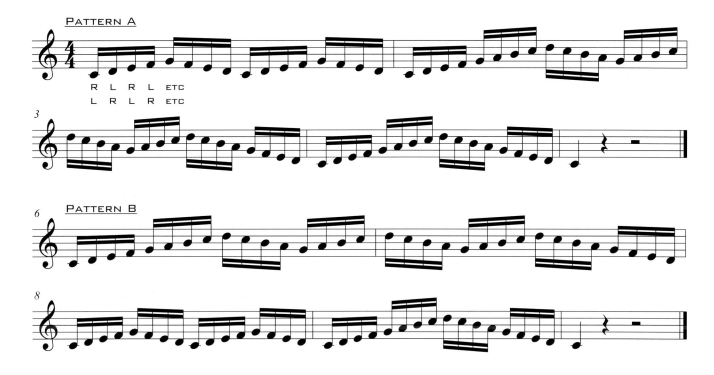

Pattern A

R L R L ETC
L R L R ETC

Pattern B

## CONTINUE THROUGH ALL KEYS USING THE ABOVE PATTERNS:

_____ F

_____ B FLAT

_____ E FLAT

_____ A FLAT

_____ D FLAT

_____ G FLAT

_____ G

_____ D

_____ A

_____ E

_____ B

*4-31*

# Mallets:
## Arpeggios

C Major

L R L R L R L R  L R L R L R L R  L R L R L R L R  L R L R L R L R

F Major

L R L R L

B Flat Major

L R L R L

## Continue through all keys using the above pattern:

_____ E Flat

_____ A Flat

_____ D Flat

_____ G Flat

_____ G

_____ D

_____ A

_____ E

_____ B

*4-32*

# Mallets:
## 2 Mallets #1

**Two Octave Long**

**Scales and Arpeggios**

**Thirds**

**More Green**

*4-33*

# Mallets:
# 2 Mallets #2

**Cara's Favorite**

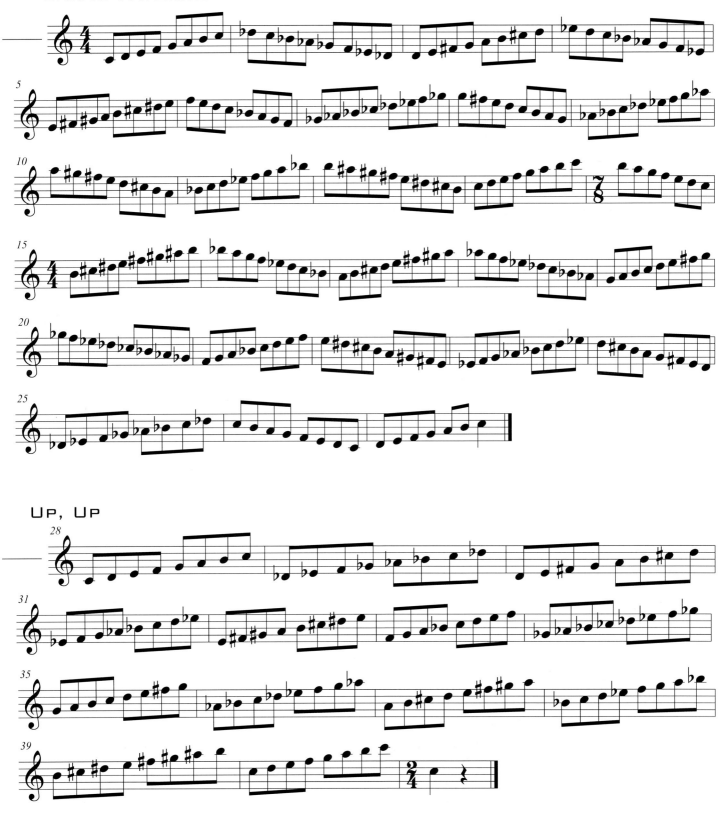

**Up, Up**

# Mallets:
# 2 Mallets #3

**Down, Down**

**Down, Up**

**Up, Down**

*4-35*

# Four on the Floor

- Grip

    -Stevens: used for better interval control, strong inner mallet independence, good for a variety of roll options; similar to traditional snare grip

    ### Stevens Grip Checklist:

    - "The thumb is always on top"
    - Commit to the curve of the Anchor Fingers: Pinky & Ring (outer mallet), and Middle (inner mallet).
    - Place the butt of the inner mallet under the thumb (not past it)
    - Do not hide the first finger. It should remain separated from the three anchor fingers
    - maintain a natural curve of the hand, no tension present

- Fundamental Strokes

>Vertical: 2 Mallets on 1 Hand at the same time; a one-handed double stop

    - the motion is a "wrist pop"
    - the fulcrum is the center of the hand
    - the mallet heads go down while the wrist comes up
    - maximum velocity to create proper sound quality
    - mallets must remain level to create a correct double stop (no flams)

> DOUBLE VERTICAL: 2 VERTICALS AT THE SAME TIME; ALL FOUR MALLETS HIT TOGETHER

> INDEPENDENT: 1 MALLET PLAYS BY ITSELF

- THE MOTION IS A "ROTATION"
- THE MALLET BEING USED WILL ROTATE AROUND THE OTHER MALLET ON THE SAME HAND; THIS OTHER MALLET SERVES AS THE AXIS OF THE MOTION
- THE MALLET NOT BEING USED NEEDS TO REMAIN STILL ENOUGH THAT IS DOES NOT STRIKE THE KEYBOARD
- CAN BE USED FOR ALTERNATING BETWEEN HANDS OR A REPETITIVE NOTE PLAYED ON A SINGLE MALLET

> ALTERNATING INDEPENDENCE:

- PERMUTATIONS PERFORMED BY SWITCHING FROM ONE MALLET TO ANOTHER
- CAN BE ALTERNATING HANDS OR ON THE SAME HAND
- EXAMPLES:

| 1 – 2 – 3 – 4 | 1 – 3 – 2 – 4 |
| 3 – 2 – 4 – 1 | 4 – 2 – 3 – 1 |
| 4 – 3 – 2 – 1 | ETC... |

- ANY PATTERN THAT USES THE "ROTATIONAL" MOTION OF THE INDEPENDENT STROKE

> LATERALS: 2 MALLETS ON 1 HAND STRIKE IN QUICK SECESSION AS ONE MOTION; THE "ONE-HANDED FLAM"

- THE MOTION IS A "ROTATION"
- THE SOUND IS SIMILAR TO AN OPEN FLAM

- USED FOR:
    - HIGH VELOCITY PERMUTATIONS
    - "LATERAL ROLLS"
    - EXAMPLES:

$$1 - 2 - 4 - 3 \quad 3 - 4 - 2 - 1$$

$$4 - 3 - 1 - 2 \quad 2 - 1 - 3 - 4$$

$$3 - 4 - 1 - 2 \quad \text{ETC...}$$

    - STICKINGS ARE SIMILAR TO A DOUBLE-STROKE ROLL

- ## ADDITIONAL STROKES

    >ONE HANDED ROLL: RAPID AND SMOOTH ALTERNATING BETWEEN MALLETS ON THE SAME HAND
        - THE MOTION IS A "ROTATION"
        - PLAYED AS:
            - METERED (A DEFINED RHYTHM)
                        OR
            - NON-METERED (NO DEFINED RHYTHM)

    >TRIPLE LATERAL: A SEQUENCE OF THREE HITS ON ONE HAND
        - THE MOTION IS A "ROTATION"
        - EXAMPLES:

$$1\text{-}2\text{-}1 - 3\text{-}4\text{-}3$$

$$2\text{-}1\text{-}2 - 4\text{-}3\text{-}4$$

$$3\text{-}4\text{-}3 - 2\text{-}1\text{-}2$$

                            ETC.....

# Mallets:
# 4 on the Floor — permutations

| Double Lateral | Single Alternating | Mirror Double Lateral |
|---|---|---|
| 1 2 3 4 | 1 3 2 4 | 1 3 4 2 |
| 2 3 4 1 | 3 2 4 1 | 3 4 2 1 |
| 3 4 1 2 | 2 4 1 3 | 4 2 1 3 |
| 4 1 2 3 | 4 1 3 2 | 2 1 3 4 |
| 4 3 2 1 | 4 2 3 1 | 2 4 3 1 |
| 1 4 3 2 | 1 4 2 3 | 1 2 4 3 |
| 2 1 4 3 | 3 1 4 2 | 3 1 2 4 |
| 3 2 1 4 | 2 3 1 4 | 4 3 1 2 |

>Improve one permutation from each column at each practice session

>At the same tempo play each permutation as:

> -Eighth notes

> -Triplets

> -Sixteenth notes

> -Sixtuplets

> -32$^{nd}$ notes

>The more permutations you master, the better a player you will be...

# Mallets:
## 4 Mallet Exercises - 1

Wharton's Special

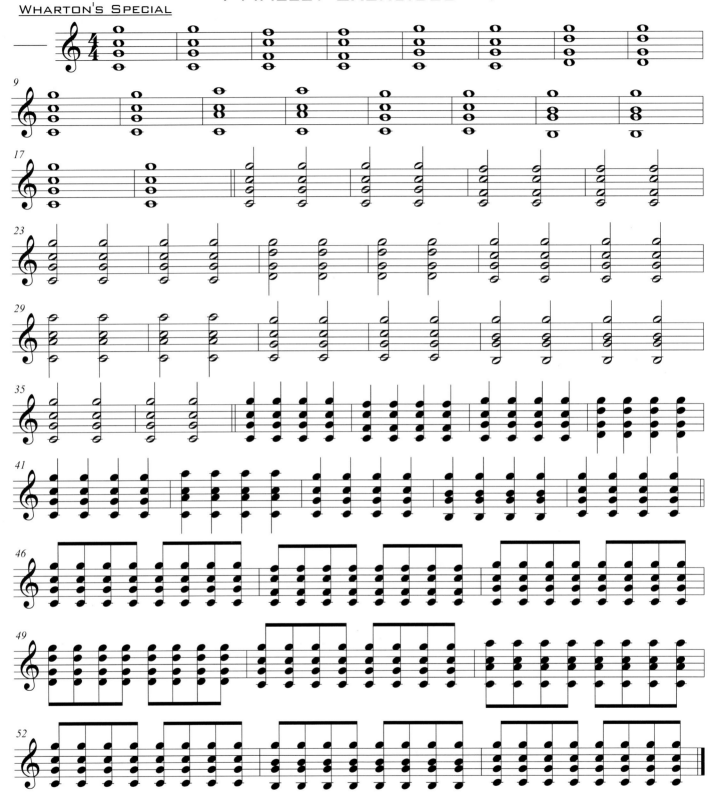

*Variations: -play with all permutations (lateral, alternating, etc)
-play with all dynamics
-divide hands into verticals vs. permtuations
-play with windshield wiper variations
-play in all major and minor keys and modes

*4-40*

# Mallets:
# 4 Mallet Exercises - 2

*Verticals: Single/Double

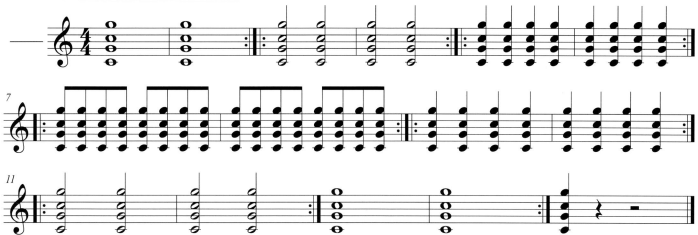

*Playing Options:
1. Play with one hand only/ two hands
2. Play at a variety of intervals:
   > C - G: 5th
   > C - F: 4th
   > C - A: 6th
   > etc...
3. Alternate interavls on each hit and/or measure

**Independence

**Playing Options:
1. Play as written
2. Play at a variety of intervals:
3. Play as double stops:
   > 2/3
   > 1/4
4. Alternate the double stops

*4-41*

# Mallets:
## 4 Mallet Exercises - 3

**\*Permutations:**

1 2 3 4 1 2 3 4   1 2 3 4 1 2 3 4      1 3 2 4 1 3 2 4   1 3 2 4 1 3 2 4

1 4 3 2 1 4 3 2   1 4 3 2 1 4 3 2      1 2 4 3 1 2 4 3   1 2 4 3 1 2 4 3

1 3 4 2 1 3 4 2   1 3 4 2 1 3 4 2      1 4 2 3 1 4 2 3   1 4 2 3 1 4 2 3

**\*Playing Options:**
1. Play at a variety of intervals:
   - \> C - G: 5th
   - \> C - F: 4th
   - \> C - A: 6th
   - \> etc...
2. Start on a different mallet
3. See "Four on The Floor" for all permutations

**\*\*Windshield Wipers:**

1/3 2/4  1/3 2/4  1/3 2/4  1/3 2/4   etc.

**\*\*Playing Options:**
Use a variety of keys with all wiper combinations

_____   1/3 - 2/4

_____   2/3 - 1/4

_____   1/4 - 2/3

_____   2/4 - 1/3

**4-42**

# Mallets:
## 4 Mallet Exercises - 4

**Double Verticals - Major Chords**

**\*Permutated Arpeggios**

\*Playing Options:

- perform with all sticking permutations:
  example: 4 - 3 - 2 - 1 / 1 - 2 - 3 - 4

-This will change the order of the pitches within the arpeggios

-see " Four on the Floor" for all permutations

*4-43*

# Mallets:
# 4 Mallet Exercises - 5

*<u>One-Handed Roll: rhythmic workout</u>

1/3   2/4   1/3   2/4   ETC

*Playing Options:

- perform at all intervals

-Add a vertical stroke in the opposite hand

**<u>Lateral Rolls Builders</u>

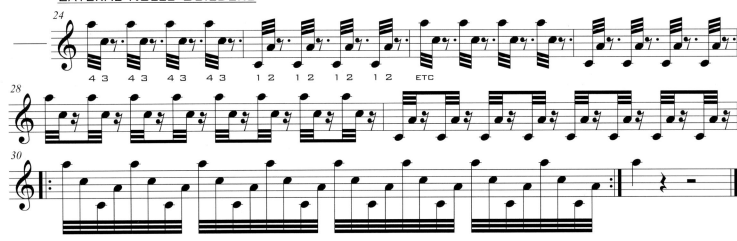

4 3   4 3   4 3   4 3   1 2   1 2   1 2   1 2   ETC

**Playing Options:

- Perform with a variety of intervals

- Use all of the Lateral sticking permutations

*4-44*

©feciv

# Mallets:
# 4 Mallet Exercises - 6

*Double Verticals

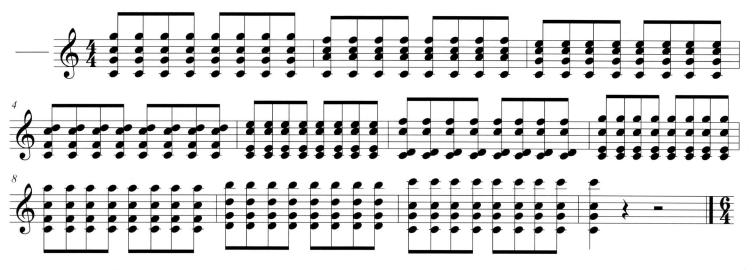

*Playing Options:

-Perform in all keys

-perform as alternating permutations
(See the "four on the Floor" section)

**Triple laterals

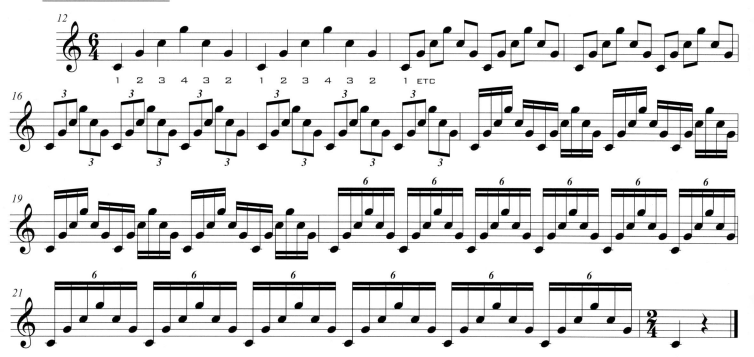

**Playing Options:

- perform with all intervals and keys

- perform with all permutations
    -This will change the order of the pitches within the patterns
    -see "Four on the Floor" for all permutations

**4-45**

# SECTION FIVE

# DRUMSET

# DRUMSET:
## ROLL CALL

ROLL CALL IS AN INTRODUCTORY EXERCISE USED TO DEVELOP A FOUR LIMB APPROACH TO DRUMSET. A SET RHYTHM IS USED TO MOVE THROUGH THE FOUR LIMBS IN A SEQUENCE OF COUNTS AND/OR MEASURES.

THE FOCUS OF THE PLAYING DURING ROLL CALL IS:
- CONSISTENT TEMPO/RHYTHM
- BALANCE OF VOLUMES TO THE RIDE CYM
- CORRECT TECHNIQUE
- MAINTAINING PLACEMENT WITHIN THE SEQUENCE
- USING CORRECT LIMB
- STAYING RELAXED AND COMFORTABLE

*ROLL CALL RHYTHMS*

THERE ARE SEVERAL SEQUENCES USED FOR PERFORMING ROLL CALL:
1. MEASURES ADD ON:
    - START WITH A LOWER NUMBER OF MEASURES PER LIMB AND THEN ADD ONE EACH SEQUENCE TO DEVELOP ENDURANCE
2. MEASURES SUBTRACTION:
    - START WITH A HIGHER NUMBER OF MEASURES PER LIMB AND TAKE ONE AWAY EACH SEQUENCE TO DEVELOP FLUIDITY
3. COUNTS SUBTRACTION:
    - START WITH 8 COUNTS PER LIMB AND THEN TAKE AWAY ONE COUNT EACH SEQUENCE UNTIL PLAYING ONE HIT PER LIMB.

*ROLL CALL QUARTER NOTES - MEASURES SUBTRACTION*

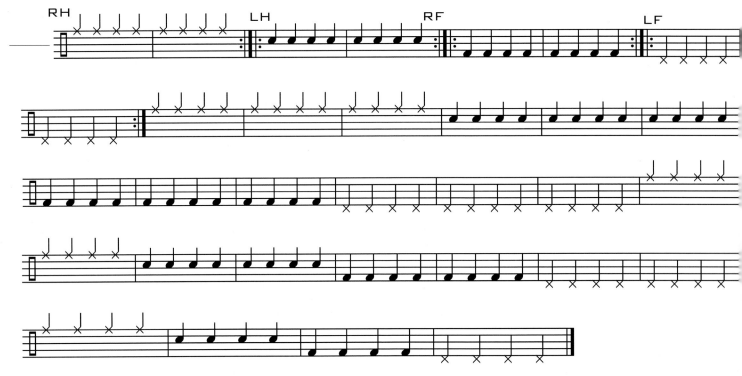

*5-1*

*ROLL CALL 8TH NOTES - COUNTS SUBTRACTION*

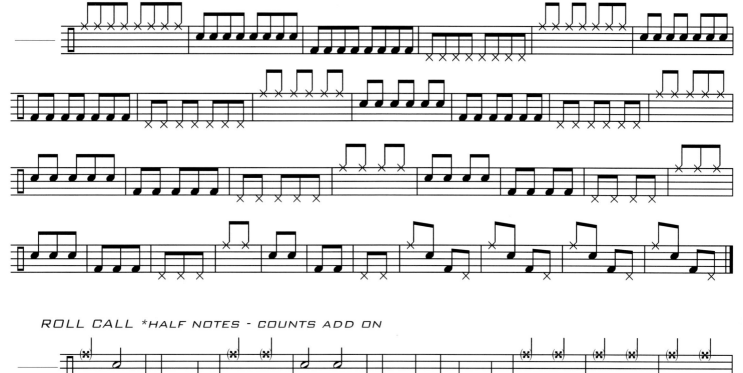

*ROLL CALL \*HALF NOTES - COUNTS ADD ON*

\*USE NOTES WITH "MORE SPACE" TO DEVELOP PATIENCE. CONCENTRATE ON THE SUBDIVISIONS BETWEEN NOTES

*ROLL CALL \*\*16TH NOTES - COUNTS ADD ON*

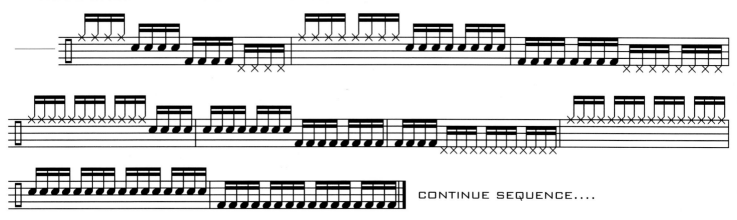

CONTINUE SEQUENCE....

\*\*USE FASTER RHYTHMS TO DEVELOP SPEED AND ENDURANCE

THE NEXT STEP OF ROLL CALL IS THE *OVERLAPPING ROLL CALL* VARIATION.
THIS FORM OF ROLL CALL IS ACHIEVED WITH LAYERING THE LIMBS IN PAIRS AND/OR TRIOS
BY TAKING THE NEXT LIMB IN THE SEQUENCE AND ADDING IT TO THE CURRENT LIMB:

HERE IS THE "STOCK" LIMB SEQUENCE OF RH - LH - RF - LF IN AN *OVERLAPPING
ROLL CALL* FORMAT:

RH/LH - LH/RF - RF/LF - LF/RH

ANY LIMB SEQUENCE CAN BE PLAYED WITH *OVERLAPPING ROLL CALL* WHILE USING THE
COUNTS/MEASURES ADD-ON'S, SUBTRACTIONS, AND COUNTDOWNS FROM THE EARLIER
ROLL CALL PAGES.

THE MORE LIMB SEQUENCES YOU CAN INCORPORATE INTO THE OVERLAPPING ROLL CALL
CONCEPT THE MORE DEVELOPED YOUR DRUMSET INDEPENDENCE WILL BECOME.

HERE ARE SOME EXAMPLES OF 2-LIMB AND 3-LIMB VARIATIONS:

*2-LIMB OVERLAPPING ROLL CALL - COUNTDOWN 8-1*

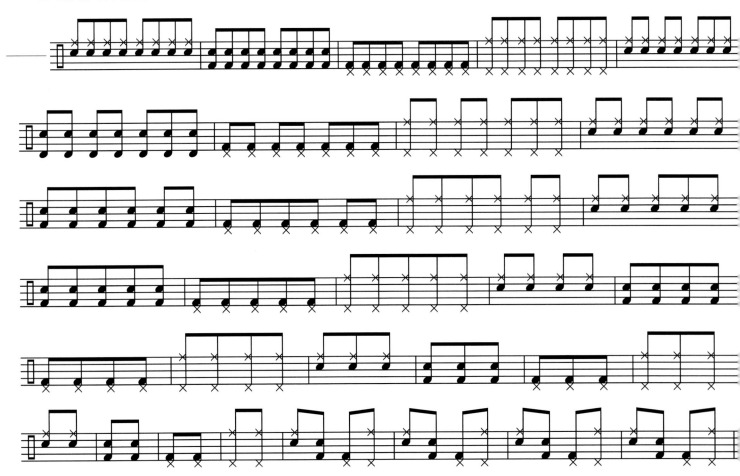

*5-3*

**3-Limb Overlapping Roll Call**

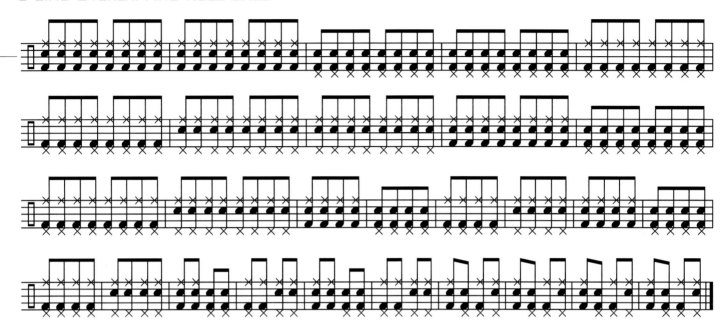

OVERLAPPING ROLL CALL CAN ALSO BE PLAYED WITH DIFFERENT RHYTHMS ON DIFFERENT LIMBS. THIS VARIATION CAN BE USED IN ANY COMBINATION OF LIMBS SO TRY AS MANY AS POSSIBLE...

THIS EXAMPLE IS A *2-Limb Overlapping Roll Call* WITH THE FOLLOWING ASSIGNMENTS:
RH: 8TH'S  LH: 8TH'S  RF: 8TH'S  LF; 1/4'S

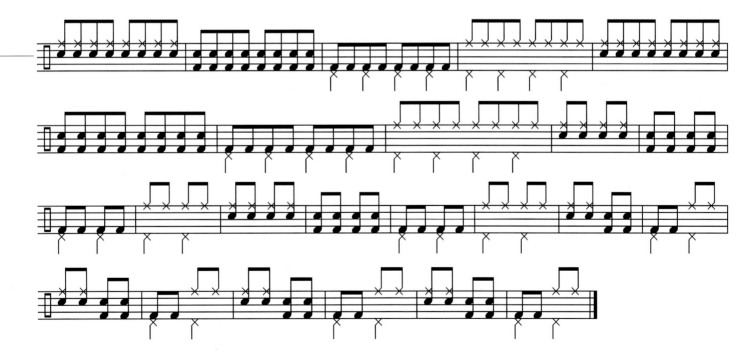

# DRUMSET:
## ROLL CALL WITH A CONSTANT

>ONCE THE ROLL CALL CONCEPT HAS BECOME COMFORTABLE, WE WILL NOW DEVELOP IT BY ADDING MORE LIMB INDEPENDENCE. THIS IS ACHIEVED BY CREATING A *CONSTANT* FOR EACH SEQUENCE.

>THE *CONSTANT* IS AN ASSIGNED LIMB THAT WILL PLAY FOR THE ENTIRE ROLL CALL SEQUENCE WHILE THE OTHER THREE LIMBS CONTINUE TO PASS THE RHYTHM AROUND THE DRUMSET.

ROLL CALL QUARTER NOTES WITH RH *CONSTANT*

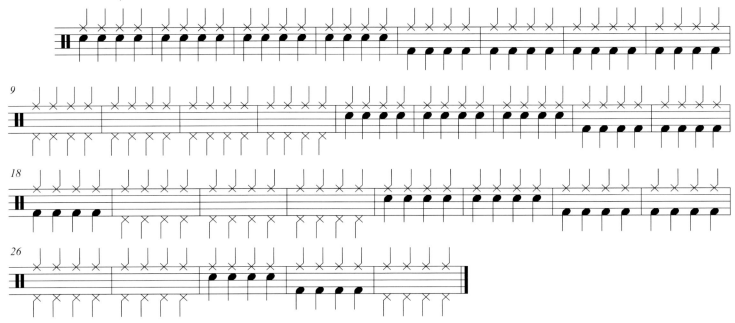

ROLL CALL 8TH NOTES WITH LH *CONSTANT*

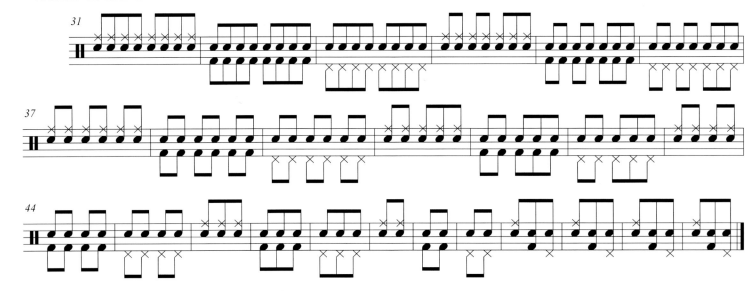

>ALSO PRACTICE THE OVERLAPPING ROLL CALL WITH THE CONSTANT LIMB CONCEPT.

5-5

# Drumset:
## Independence Grid
## Level One/Two

> The Independence Grids are used to continue the four limb coordination that was introduced in Roll Call.

> The grid is performed by selecting a rhythm for each limb. The RH and LF are played as *Constants* while the LH and RF sequence through their A-D patterns.

> The LH/RF patterns can be played by:
- Each measure repeated as its own sequence
- An entire line is played as a sequence
- Moving randomly through each line to mix up the sequence

RH (Ride Cym/ HH):

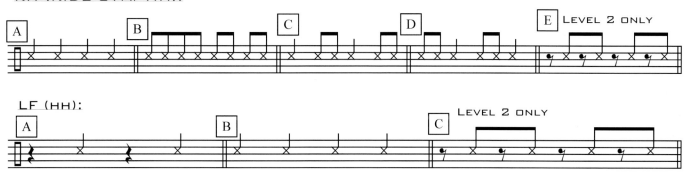

LF (HH):

*LH (Snare)/ RF (Bass) :

*Level 2: Play LH/RF A-D as "upbeats" and as 2 8th notes

5-6

# DRUMSET:
## INDEPENDENCE GRID
## LEVEL THREE/FOUR

RH (RIDE CYM)/ (HH):

LF (HH):

**LH (SNARE)/ RF (BASS) :

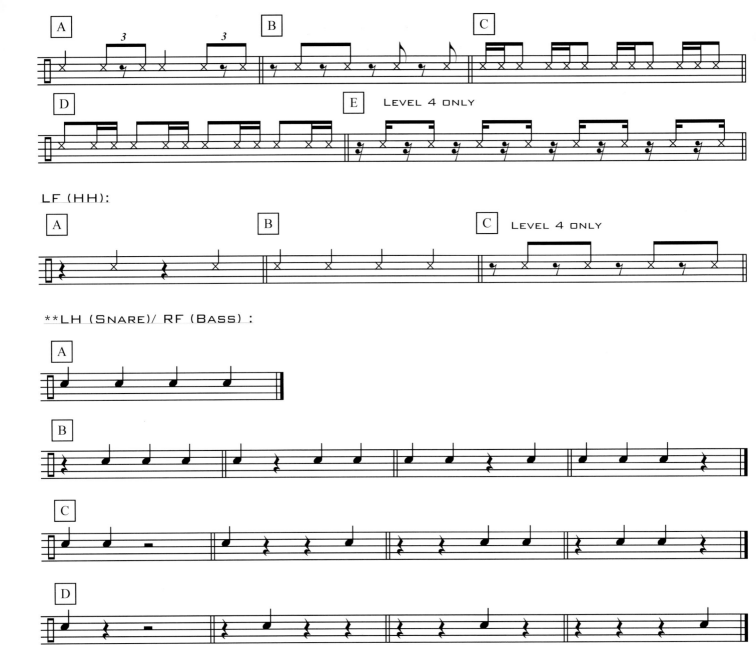

**LEVEL 4: PLAY SNARE/BASS A-D AS "UPBEATS" AND 2 8TH NOTES

EXTRA LATIN BASS PATTERNS:

A — SAMBA/BOSSA-NOVA   B — HYBRID   C — MAMBO/SONGO

5-7

# Drumset:
# 16th Note Grid

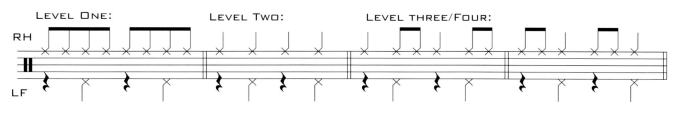

LATIN PATTERNS:

## Play each pattern Left Hand or Alternating Hands (No Cym):

## *Apply all above patterns to the following beats:

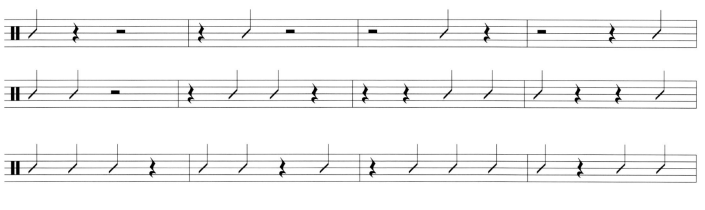

*Play: 1. each bar 4 times
2. each bar 2 times
3. play straight through

*5-8*

# Drumset:
## Triplet Grid

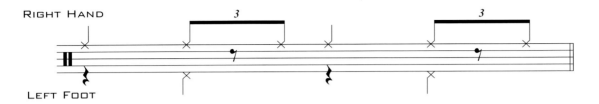

**Play each pattern as: 1. LH only  2. RF only  3. LH/RF double stop**

Level One:

Level Two:

**Play each pattern as written:**

Level Three:

Level Four:

**\*Apply all above patterns to the following beats:**

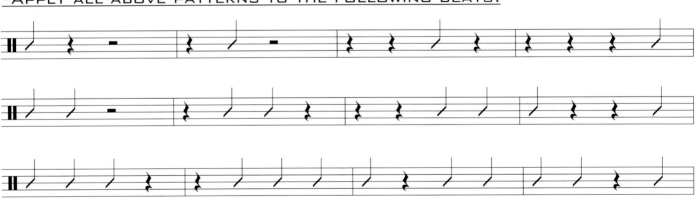

**\*Play: 1. each bar 4 times**
**2. each bar 2 times**
**3. play straight through**

*5-9*

# Applying Rhythm Sheets to Drumset

All of the pages from *Section One: Rhythm* can be applied to your daily drumset practice regimen.

By using the following six applications (or creating your own) you can:
- strengthen coordination skills
- expand orchestration of fills and solos
- increase repertoire of grooves and styles.

Be creative and have fun!!!

*****All application examples come from page 1-11, ms. 12-15*****

### Application One: Latin Feet w/ Hands Playing Rhythms

### Application Two: RH/LF Patterns with LH/RF Playing Rhythms

### Rhythm Example Split Between LH/RF

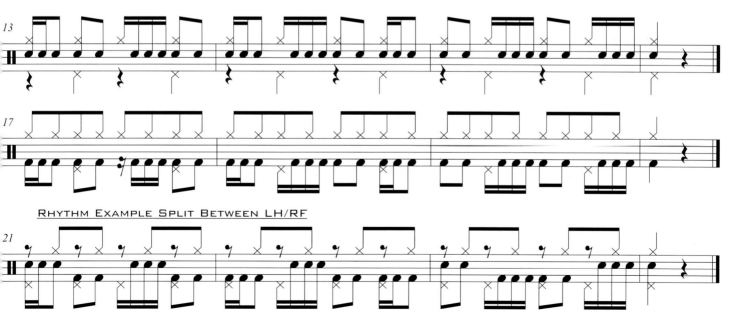

5-10

# APPLYING RHYTHM SHEETS TO DRUMSET (CONT.)

## APPLICATION THREE: SPLIT RHYTHMS BETWEEN ALL LIMBS

### RANDOM LIMB CHOICES

### SEQUENTIAL LIMB CHOICES

## APPLICATION FOUR: RHYTHM PLAYED AS A GROOVE

## APPLICATION FIVE: RHYTHM PLAYED AS SOLO/FILLS

### RHYTHM PLAYED AS SOLO

### RHYTHM PLAYED AS FILLS

# Applying Rhythm Sheets to Drumset (cont.)

> The final rhythm sheet to drumset appliations is the Swing Style. this application is essential for learning the coordination and rhythms necessary for playing any swing style. There are a few ways to do this so lets look at them:

## Application Six: Swing Style

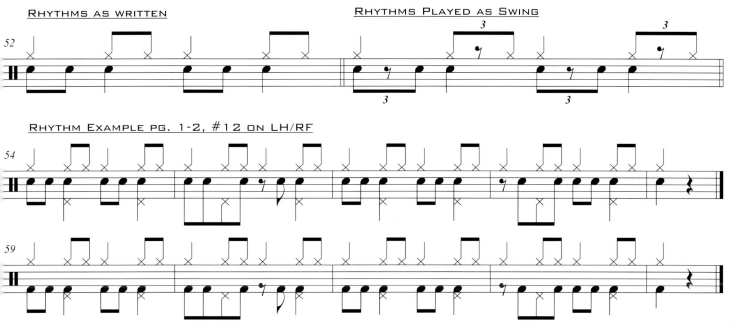

> The next example is for applying 16th note rhythms to swing. This is achieved by converting the 16th notes rhythms page into **half-time** and then playing the new rhythms in a swing style. The example below is from *Page 1-11, ms 12-15*. This is the same rhythm example used in the earlier applications (1-5).

## 16th's Rhythms Played as Swing in Half Time

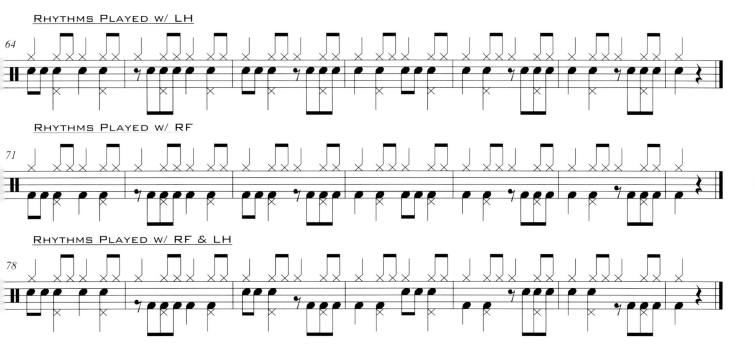

# Applying Rhythm Sheets to Drumset (cont.)

This page has two additional Applications that are considered to be more advanced level styles. Once you have successful worked through the previous 5 Applications, you should move on to these bonus applications...

### Bonus Application One: Hip Hop (swung 16th's)

RHYTHMS AS WRITTEN        RHYTHMS PLAYED AS HIP HOP

RH Playing straight pattern with hip hop LH/RF

Rhythms played as hip hop groove

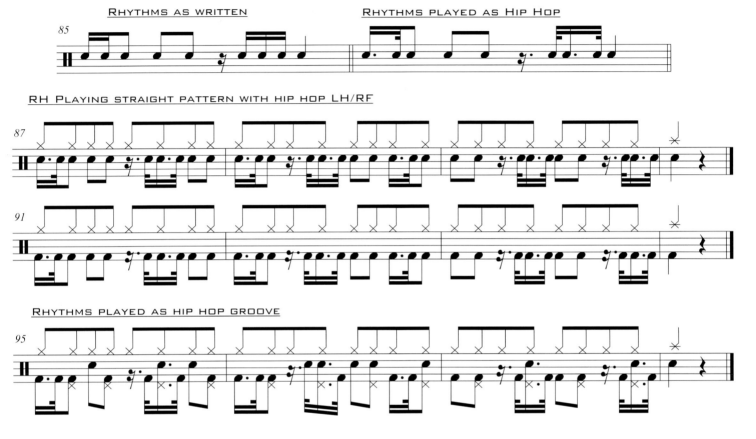

### Bonus Application two: LF Clave Patterns

> The next application involves adding a LF clave pattern to the latin RF. This can be played with both hands playing the rhythm example or with hands playing latin groove.

Left Foot Clave Pattern: 3-2

Left Foot Clave Pattern: 2-3

>Add clave LF to the other latin RF patterns as well<

5-13

# DRUMSET:
## GROOVES - LEVEL ONE/TWO

**LEVEL ONE GROOVES**

ROCK

HALF-TIME

16TH NOTE ROCK

SWING

**LEVEL TWO GROOVES**

SYNCHOPATED FUNK (JAMES BROWN)

8TH NOTE FUNK (CHAMELEON)

BOSSA NOVA

SOCA

*5-14*

# DRUMSET:
## GROOVES - LEVEL THREE/FOUR

**LEVEL THREE GROOVES**

JAZZ WALTZ (3/4)

SAMBA

JAZZ SHUFFLE

16TH NOTE R&B (STRAIGHT)/ HIP HOP (SWUNG)

**LEVEL FOUR GROOVES**

MAMBO

SONGO

NANIGO/ 12/8 WORLD GROOVE

*5-15*

# SECTION SIX

# ASSIGNMENTS
# CHARTS

# The Packet Assignments Chart

| Page | Line/Measures | Tempo | Due Date | Notes | Achieved |
|------|---------------|-------|----------|-------|----------|
| 3-16 | | 80bpm | | | |
| 3-16 | | 115bpm | | no | |
| 3-1 | | 88 | | | |
| | | | | | |
| | | | | | |
| | | | | | |
| | | | | | |
| | | | | | |
| | | | | | |
| | | | | | |
| | | | | | |
| | | | | | |
| | | | | | |
| | | | | | |
| | | | | | |
| | | | | | |
| | | | | | |
| | | | | | |
| | | | | | |
| | | | | | |
| | | | | | |
| | | | | | |
| | | | | | |
| | | | | | |
| | | | | | |
| | | | | | |
| | | | | | |
| | | | | | |
| | | | | | |
| | | | | | |
| | | | | | |
| | | | | | |
| | | | | | |
| | | | | | |
| | | | | | |
| | | | | | |
| | | | | | |
| | | | | | |
| | | | | | |
| | | | | | |
| | | | | | |
| | | | | | |
| | | | | | |

# The Packet Assignments Chart

| Page | Line/Measures | Tempo | Due Date | Notes | Achieved |
|------|---------------|-------|----------|-------|----------|
|      |               |       |          |       |          |
|      |               |       |          |       |          |
|      |               |       |          |       |          |
|      |               |       |          |       |          |
|      |               |       |          |       |          |
|      |               |       |          |       |          |
|      |               |       |          |       |          |
|      |               |       |          |       |          |
|      |               |       |          |       |          |
|      |               |       |          |       |          |
|      |               |       |          |       |          |
|      |               |       |          |       |          |
|      |               |       |          |       |          |
|      |               |       |          |       |          |
|      |               |       |          |       |          |
|      |               |       |          |       |          |
|      |               |       |          |       |          |
|      |               |       |          |       |          |
|      |               |       |          |       |          |
|      |               |       |          |       |          |
|      |               |       |          |       |          |
|      |               |       |          |       |          |
|      |               |       |          |       |          |
|      |               |       |          |       |          |
|      |               |       |          |       |          |
|      |               |       |          |       |          |
|      |               |       |          |       |          |
|      |               |       |          |       |          |
|      |               |       |          |       |          |
|      |               |       |          |       |          |
|      |               |       |          |       |          |
|      |               |       |          |       |          |
|      |               |       |          |       |          |
|      |               |       |          |       |          |
|      |               |       |          |       |          |
|      |               |       |          |       |          |
|      |               |       |          |       |          |
|      |               |       |          |       |          |
|      |               |       |          |       |          |
|      |               |       |          |       |          |

# THE PACKET ASSIGNMENTS CHART

| Page | Line/Measures | Tempo | Due Date | Notes | Achieved |
|------|---------------|-------|----------|-------|----------|
|      |               |       |          |       |          |
|      |               |       |          |       |          |
|      |               |       |          |       |          |
|      |               |       |          |       |          |
|      |               |       |          |       |          |
|      |               |       |          |       |          |
|      |               |       |          |       |          |
|      |               |       |          |       |          |
|      |               |       |          |       |          |
|      |               |       |          |       |          |
|      |               |       |          |       |          |
|      |               |       |          |       |          |
|      |               |       |          |       |          |
|      |               |       |          |       |          |
|      |               |       |          |       |          |
|      |               |       |          |       |          |
|      |               |       |          |       |          |
|      |               |       |          |       |          |
|      |               |       |          |       |          |
|      |               |       |          |       |          |
|      |               |       |          |       |          |
|      |               |       |          |       |          |
|      |               |       |          |       |          |
|      |               |       |          |       |          |
|      |               |       |          |       |          |
|      |               |       |          |       |          |
|      |               |       |          |       |          |
|      |               |       |          |       |          |
|      |               |       |          |       |          |
|      |               |       |          |       |          |
|      |               |       |          |       |          |
|      |               |       |          |       |          |
|      |               |       |          |       |          |
|      |               |       |          |       |          |
|      |               |       |          |       |          |
|      |               |       |          |       |          |
|      |               |       |          |       |          |
|      |               |       |          |       |          |
|      |               |       |          |       |          |
|      |               |       |          |       |          |

# The Packet Assignments Chart

| Page | Line/Measures | Tempo | Due Date | Notes | Achieved |
|------|---------------|-------|----------|-------|----------|
|      |               |       |          |       |          |
|      |               |       |          |       |          |
|      |               |       |          |       |          |
|      |               |       |          |       |          |
|      |               |       |          |       |          |
|      |               |       |          |       |          |
|      |               |       |          |       |          |
|      |               |       |          |       |          |
|      |               |       |          |       |          |
|      |               |       |          |       |          |
|      |               |       |          |       |          |
|      |               |       |          |       |          |
|      |               |       |          |       |          |
|      |               |       |          |       |          |
|      |               |       |          |       |          |
|      |               |       |          |       |          |
|      |               |       |          |       |          |
|      |               |       |          |       |          |
|      |               |       |          |       |          |
|      |               |       |          |       |          |
|      |               |       |          |       |          |
|      |               |       |          |       |          |
|      |               |       |          |       |          |
|      |               |       |          |       |          |
|      |               |       |          |       |          |
|      |               |       |          |       |          |
|      |               |       |          |       |          |
|      |               |       |          |       |          |
|      |               |       |          |       |          |
|      |               |       |          |       |          |
|      |               |       |          |       |          |
|      |               |       |          |       |          |
|      |               |       |          |       |          |
|      |               |       |          |       |          |
|      |               |       |          |       |          |
|      |               |       |          |       |          |
|      |               |       |          |       |          |
|      |               |       |          |       |          |
|      |               |       |          |       |          |
|      |               |       |          |       |          |
|      |               |       |          |       |          |

# The Packet Assignments Chart

| Page | Line/Measures | Tempo | Due Date | Notes | Achieved |
|------|---------------|-------|----------|-------|----------|
|      |               |       |          |       |          |
|      |               |       |          |       |          |
|      |               |       |          |       |          |
|      |               |       |          |       |          |
|      |               |       |          |       |          |
|      |               |       |          |       |          |
|      |               |       |          |       |          |
|      |               |       |          |       |          |
|      |               |       |          |       |          |
|      |               |       |          |       |          |
|      |               |       |          |       |          |
|      |               |       |          |       |          |
|      |               |       |          |       |          |
|      |               |       |          |       |          |
|      |               |       |          |       |          |
|      |               |       |          |       |          |
|      |               |       |          |       |          |
|      |               |       |          |       |          |
|      |               |       |          |       |          |
|      |               |       |          |       |          |
|      |               |       |          |       |          |
|      |               |       |          |       |          |
|      |               |       |          |       |          |
|      |               |       |          |       |          |
|      |               |       |          |       |          |
|      |               |       |          |       |          |
|      |               |       |          |       |          |
|      |               |       |          |       |          |
|      |               |       |          |       |          |
|      |               |       |          |       |          |
|      |               |       |          |       |          |
|      |               |       |          |       |          |
|      |               |       |          |       |          |
|      |               |       |          |       |          |
|      |               |       |          |       |          |
|      |               |       |          |       |          |
|      |               |       |          |       |          |
|      |               |       |          |       |          |
|      |               |       |          |       |          |

# The Packet Assignments Chart

| Page | Line/Measures | Tempo | Due Date | Notes | Achieved |
|------|---------------|-------|----------|-------|----------|
|      |               |       |          |       |          |
|      |               |       |          |       |          |
|      |               |       |          |       |          |
|      |               |       |          |       |          |
|      |               |       |          |       |          |
|      |               |       |          |       |          |
|      |               |       |          |       |          |
|      |               |       |          |       |          |
|      |               |       |          |       |          |
|      |               |       |          |       |          |
|      |               |       |          |       |          |
|      |               |       |          |       |          |
|      |               |       |          |       |          |
|      |               |       |          |       |          |
|      |               |       |          |       |          |
|      |               |       |          |       |          |
|      |               |       |          |       |          |
|      |               |       |          |       |          |
|      |               |       |          |       |          |
|      |               |       |          |       |          |
|      |               |       |          |       |          |
|      |               |       |          |       |          |
|      |               |       |          |       |          |
|      |               |       |          |       |          |
|      |               |       |          |       |          |
|      |               |       |          |       |          |
|      |               |       |          |       |          |
|      |               |       |          |       |          |
|      |               |       |          |       |          |
|      |               |       |          |       |          |
|      |               |       |          |       |          |
|      |               |       |          |       |          |
|      |               |       |          |       |          |
|      |               |       |          |       |          |
|      |               |       |          |       |          |
|      |               |       |          |       |          |
|      |               |       |          |       |          |
|      |               |       |          |       |          |
|      |               |       |          |       |          |
|      |               |       |          |       |          |

# The Packet Assignments Chart

| Page | Line/Measures | Tempo | Due Date | Notes | Achieved |
|------|---------------|-------|----------|-------|----------|
|      |               |       |          |       |          |
|      |               |       |          |       |          |
|      |               |       |          |       |          |
|      |               |       |          |       |          |
|      |               |       |          |       |          |
|      |               |       |          |       |          |
|      |               |       |          |       |          |
|      |               |       |          |       |          |
|      |               |       |          |       |          |
|      |               |       |          |       |          |
|      |               |       |          |       |          |
|      |               |       |          |       |          |
|      |               |       |          |       |          |
|      |               |       |          |       |          |
|      |               |       |          |       |          |
|      |               |       |          |       |          |
|      |               |       |          |       |          |
|      |               |       |          |       |          |
|      |               |       |          |       |          |
|      |               |       |          |       |          |
|      |               |       |          |       |          |
|      |               |       |          |       |          |
|      |               |       |          |       |          |
|      |               |       |          |       |          |
|      |               |       |          |       |          |
|      |               |       |          |       |          |
|      |               |       |          |       |          |
|      |               |       |          |       |          |
|      |               |       |          |       |          |
|      |               |       |          |       |          |
|      |               |       |          |       |          |
|      |               |       |          |       |          |
|      |               |       |          |       |          |
|      |               |       |          |       |          |
|      |               |       |          |       |          |
|      |               |       |          |       |          |
|      |               |       |          |       |          |
|      |               |       |          |       |          |
|      |               |       |          |       |          |

# The Packet Assignments Chart

| Page | Line/Measures | Tempo | Due Date | Notes | Achieved |
|------|---------------|-------|----------|-------|----------|
|  |  |  |  |  |  |
|  |  |  |  |  |  |
|  |  |  |  |  |  |
|  |  |  |  |  |  |
|  |  |  |  |  |  |
|  |  |  |  |  |  |
|  |  |  |  |  |  |
|  |  |  |  |  |  |
|  |  |  |  |  |  |
|  |  |  |  |  |  |
|  |  |  |  |  |  |
|  |  |  |  |  |  |
|  |  |  |  |  |  |
|  |  |  |  |  |  |
|  |  |  |  |  |  |
|  |  |  |  |  |  |
|  |  |  |  |  |  |
|  |  |  |  |  |  |
|  |  |  |  |  |  |
|  |  |  |  |  |  |
|  |  |  |  |  |  |
|  |  |  |  |  |  |
|  |  |  |  |  |  |
|  |  |  |  |  |  |
|  |  |  |  |  |  |
|  |  |  |  |  |  |
|  |  |  |  |  |  |
|  |  |  |  |  |  |
|  |  |  |  |  |  |
|  |  |  |  |  |  |
|  |  |  |  |  |  |
|  |  |  |  |  |  |
|  |  |  |  |  |  |
|  |  |  |  |  |  |
|  |  |  |  |  |  |
|  |  |  |  |  |  |
|  |  |  |  |  |  |
|  |  |  |  |  |  |
|  |  |  |  |  |  |
|  |  |  |  |  |  |

# The Packet Assignments Chart

| Page | Line/Measures | Tempo | Due Date | Notes | Achieved |
|------|---------------|-------|----------|-------|----------|
|      |               |       |          |       |          |
|      |               |       |          |       |          |
|      |               |       |          |       |          |
|      |               |       |          |       |          |
|      |               |       |          |       |          |
|      |               |       |          |       |          |
|      |               |       |          |       |          |
|      |               |       |          |       |          |
|      |               |       |          |       |          |
|      |               |       |          |       |          |
|      |               |       |          |       |          |
|      |               |       |          |       |          |
|      |               |       |          |       |          |
|      |               |       |          |       |          |
|      |               |       |          |       |          |
|      |               |       |          |       |          |
|      |               |       |          |       |          |
|      |               |       |          |       |          |
|      |               |       |          |       |          |
|      |               |       |          |       |          |
|      |               |       |          |       |          |
|      |               |       |          |       |          |
|      |               |       |          |       |          |
|      |               |       |          |       |          |
|      |               |       |          |       |          |
|      |               |       |          |       |          |
|      |               |       |          |       |          |
|      |               |       |          |       |          |
|      |               |       |          |       |          |
|      |               |       |          |       |          |
|      |               |       |          |       |          |
|      |               |       |          |       |          |
|      |               |       |          |       |          |
|      |               |       |          |       |          |
|      |               |       |          |       |          |
|      |               |       |          |       |          |
|      |               |       |          |       |          |

# The Packet Assignments Chart

| Page | Line/Measures | Tempo | Due Date | Notes | Achieved |
|------|--------------|-------|----------|-------|----------|
|      |              |       |          |       |          |
|      |              |       |          |       |          |
|      |              |       |          |       |          |
|      |              |       |          |       |          |
|      |              |       |          |       |          |
|      |              |       |          |       |          |
|      |              |       |          |       |          |
|      |              |       |          |       |          |
|      |              |       |          |       |          |
|      |              |       |          |       |          |
|      |              |       |          |       |          |
|      |              |       |          |       |          |
|      |              |       |          |       |          |
|      |              |       |          |       |          |
|      |              |       |          |       |          |
|      |              |       |          |       |          |
|      |              |       |          |       |          |
|      |              |       |          |       |          |
|      |              |       |          |       |          |
|      |              |       |          |       |          |
|      |              |       |          |       |          |
|      |              |       |          |       |          |
|      |              |       |          |       |          |
|      |              |       |          |       |          |
|      |              |       |          |       |          |
|      |              |       |          |       |          |
|      |              |       |          |       |          |
|      |              |       |          |       |          |
|      |              |       |          |       |          |
|      |              |       |          |       |          |
|      |              |       |          |       |          |
|      |              |       |          |       |          |
|      |              |       |          |       |          |
|      |              |       |          |       |          |
|      |              |       |          |       |          |
|      |              |       |          |       |          |
|      |              |       |          |       |          |
|      |              |       |          |       |          |
|      |              |       |          |       |          |
|      |              |       |          |       |          |

# The Packet Assignments Chart

| Page | Line/Measures | Tempo | Due Date | Notes | Achieved |
|------|---------------|-------|----------|-------|----------|
|      |               |       |          |       |          |
|      |               |       |          |       |          |
|      |               |       |          |       |          |
|      |               |       |          |       |          |
|      |               |       |          |       |          |
|      |               |       |          |       |          |
|      |               |       |          |       |          |
|      |               |       |          |       |          |
|      |               |       |          |       |          |
|      |               |       |          |       |          |
|      |               |       |          |       |          |
|      |               |       |          |       |          |
|      |               |       |          |       |          |
|      |               |       |          |       |          |
|      |               |       |          |       |          |
|      |               |       |          |       |          |
|      |               |       |          |       |          |
|      |               |       |          |       |          |
|      |               |       |          |       |          |
|      |               |       |          |       |          |
|      |               |       |          |       |          |
|      |               |       |          |       |          |
|      |               |       |          |       |          |
|      |               |       |          |       |          |
|      |               |       |          |       |          |
|      |               |       |          |       |          |
|      |               |       |          |       |          |
|      |               |       |          |       |          |
|      |               |       |          |       |          |
|      |               |       |          |       |          |
|      |               |       |          |       |          |
|      |               |       |          |       |          |
|      |               |       |          |       |          |
|      |               |       |          |       |          |
|      |               |       |          |       |          |
|      |               |       |          |       |          |
|      |               |       |          |       |          |
|      |               |       |          |       |          |
|      |               |       |          |       |          |
|      |               |       |          |       |          |

# The Packet Assignments Chart

| Page | Line/Measures | Tempo | Due Date | Notes | Achieved |
|------|---------------|-------|----------|-------|----------|
|      |               |       |          |       |          |
|      |               |       |          |       |          |
|      |               |       |          |       |          |
|      |               |       |          |       |          |
|      |               |       |          |       |          |
|      |               |       |          |       |          |
|      |               |       |          |       |          |
|      |               |       |          |       |          |
|      |               |       |          |       |          |
|      |               |       |          |       |          |
|      |               |       |          |       |          |
|      |               |       |          |       |          |
|      |               |       |          |       |          |
|      |               |       |          |       |          |
|      |               |       |          |       |          |
|      |               |       |          |       |          |
|      |               |       |          |       |          |
|      |               |       |          |       |          |
|      |               |       |          |       |          |
|      |               |       |          |       |          |
|      |               |       |          |       |          |
|      |               |       |          |       |          |
|      |               |       |          |       |          |
|      |               |       |          |       |          |
|      |               |       |          |       |          |
|      |               |       |          |       |          |
|      |               |       |          |       |          |
|      |               |       |          |       |          |
|      |               |       |          |       |          |
|      |               |       |          |       |          |
|      |               |       |          |       |          |
|      |               |       |          |       |          |
|      |               |       |          |       |          |
|      |               |       |          |       |          |
|      |               |       |          |       |          |
|      |               |       |          |       |          |
|      |               |       |          |       |          |
|      |               |       |          |       |          |
|      |               |       |          |       |          |
|      |               |       |          |       |          |
|      |               |       |          |       |          |

# The Packet Assignments Chart

| Page | Line/Measures | Tempo | Due Date | Notes | Achieved |
|------|---------------|-------|----------|-------|----------|
|      |               |       |          |       |          |
|      |               |       |          |       |          |
|      |               |       |          |       |          |
|      |               |       |          |       |          |
|      |               |       |          |       |          |
|      |               |       |          |       |          |
|      |               |       |          |       |          |
|      |               |       |          |       |          |
|      |               |       |          |       |          |
|      |               |       |          |       |          |
|      |               |       |          |       |          |
|      |               |       |          |       |          |
|      |               |       |          |       |          |
|      |               |       |          |       |          |
|      |               |       |          |       |          |
|      |               |       |          |       |          |
|      |               |       |          |       |          |
|      |               |       |          |       |          |
|      |               |       |          |       |          |
|      |               |       |          |       |          |
|      |               |       |          |       |          |
|      |               |       |          |       |          |
|      |               |       |          |       |          |
|      |               |       |          |       |          |
|      |               |       |          |       |          |
|      |               |       |          |       |          |
|      |               |       |          |       |          |
|      |               |       |          |       |          |
|      |               |       |          |       |          |
|      |               |       |          |       |          |
|      |               |       |          |       |          |
|      |               |       |          |       |          |
|      |               |       |          |       |          |
|      |               |       |          |       |          |
|      |               |       |          |       |          |
|      |               |       |          |       |          |
|      |               |       |          |       |          |
|      |               |       |          |       |          |
|      |               |       |          |       |          |
|      |               |       |          |       |          |

# The Packet Assignments Chart

| Page | Line/Measures | Tempo | Due Date | Notes | Achieved |
|------|---------------|-------|----------|-------|----------|
|      |               |       |          |       |          |
|      |               |       |          |       |          |
|      |               |       |          |       |          |
|      |               |       |          |       |          |
|      |               |       |          |       |          |
|      |               |       |          |       |          |
|      |               |       |          |       |          |
|      |               |       |          |       |          |
|      |               |       |          |       |          |
|      |               |       |          |       |          |
|      |               |       |          |       |          |
|      |               |       |          |       |          |
|      |               |       |          |       |          |
|      |               |       |          |       |          |
|      |               |       |          |       |          |
|      |               |       |          |       |          |
|      |               |       |          |       |          |
|      |               |       |          |       |          |
|      |               |       |          |       |          |
|      |               |       |          |       |          |
|      |               |       |          |       |          |
|      |               |       |          |       |          |
|      |               |       |          |       |          |
|      |               |       |          |       |          |
|      |               |       |          |       |          |
|      |               |       |          |       |          |
|      |               |       |          |       |          |
|      |               |       |          |       |          |
|      |               |       |          |       |          |
|      |               |       |          |       |          |
|      |               |       |          |       |          |
|      |               |       |          |       |          |
|      |               |       |          |       |          |
|      |               |       |          |       |          |
|      |               |       |          |       |          |
|      |               |       |          |       |          |
|      |               |       |          |       |          |
|      |               |       |          |       |          |
|      |               |       |          |       |          |

# The Packet Assignments Chart

| Page | Line/Measures | Tempo | Due Date | Notes | Achieved |
|------|---------------|-------|----------|-------|----------|
|      |               |       |          |       |          |
|      |               |       |          |       |          |
|      |               |       |          |       |          |
|      |               |       |          |       |          |
|      |               |       |          |       |          |
|      |               |       |          |       |          |
|      |               |       |          |       |          |
|      |               |       |          |       |          |
|      |               |       |          |       |          |
|      |               |       |          |       |          |
|      |               |       |          |       |          |
|      |               |       |          |       |          |
|      |               |       |          |       |          |
|      |               |       |          |       |          |
|      |               |       |          |       |          |
|      |               |       |          |       |          |
|      |               |       |          |       |          |
|      |               |       |          |       |          |
|      |               |       |          |       |          |
|      |               |       |          |       |          |
|      |               |       |          |       |          |
|      |               |       |          |       |          |
|      |               |       |          |       |          |
|      |               |       |          |       |          |
|      |               |       |          |       |          |
|      |               |       |          |       |          |
|      |               |       |          |       |          |
|      |               |       |          |       |          |
|      |               |       |          |       |          |
|      |               |       |          |       |          |
|      |               |       |          |       |          |
|      |               |       |          |       |          |
|      |               |       |          |       |          |
|      |               |       |          |       |          |
|      |               |       |          |       |          |
|      |               |       |          |       |          |
|      |               |       |          |       |          |
|      |               |       |          |       |          |
|      |               |       |          |       |          |
|      |               |       |          |       |          |
|      |               |       |          |       |          |

# The Packet Assignments Chart

| Page | Line/Measures | Tempo | Due Date | Notes | Achieved |
|------|---------------|-------|----------|-------|----------|
|      |               |       |          |       |          |
|      |               |       |          |       |          |
|      |               |       |          |       |          |
|      |               |       |          |       |          |
|      |               |       |          |       |          |
|      |               |       |          |       |          |
|      |               |       |          |       |          |
|      |               |       |          |       |          |
|      |               |       |          |       |          |
|      |               |       |          |       |          |
|      |               |       |          |       |          |
|      |               |       |          |       |          |
|      |               |       |          |       |          |
|      |               |       |          |       |          |
|      |               |       |          |       |          |
|      |               |       |          |       |          |
|      |               |       |          |       |          |
|      |               |       |          |       |          |
|      |               |       |          |       |          |
|      |               |       |          |       |          |
|      |               |       |          |       |          |
|      |               |       |          |       |          |
|      |               |       |          |       |          |
|      |               |       |          |       |          |
|      |               |       |          |       |          |
|      |               |       |          |       |          |
|      |               |       |          |       |          |
|      |               |       |          |       |          |
|      |               |       |          |       |          |
|      |               |       |          |       |          |
|      |               |       |          |       |          |
|      |               |       |          |       |          |
|      |               |       |          |       |          |
|      |               |       |          |       |          |
|      |               |       |          |       |          |
|      |               |       |          |       |          |
|      |               |       |          |       |          |
|      |               |       |          |       |          |
|      |               |       |          |       |          |
|      |               |       |          |       |          |
|      |               |       |          |       |          |

# The Packet Assignments Chart

| Page | Line/Measures | Tempo | Due Date | Notes | Achieved |
|------|---------------|-------|----------|-------|----------|
|      |               |       |          |       |          |
|      |               |       |          |       |          |
|      |               |       |          |       |          |
|      |               |       |          |       |          |
|      |               |       |          |       |          |
|      |               |       |          |       |          |
|      |               |       |          |       |          |
|      |               |       |          |       |          |
|      |               |       |          |       |          |
|      |               |       |          |       |          |
|      |               |       |          |       |          |
|      |               |       |          |       |          |
|      |               |       |          |       |          |
|      |               |       |          |       |          |
|      |               |       |          |       |          |
|      |               |       |          |       |          |
|      |               |       |          |       |          |
|      |               |       |          |       |          |
|      |               |       |          |       |          |
|      |               |       |          |       |          |
|      |               |       |          |       |          |
|      |               |       |          |       |          |
|      |               |       |          |       |          |
|      |               |       |          |       |          |
|      |               |       |          |       |          |
|      |               |       |          |       |          |
|      |               |       |          |       |          |
|      |               |       |          |       |          |
|      |               |       |          |       |          |
|      |               |       |          |       |          |
|      |               |       |          |       |          |
|      |               |       |          |       |          |
|      |               |       |          |       |          |
|      |               |       |          |       |          |
|      |               |       |          |       |          |
|      |               |       |          |       |          |
|      |               |       |          |       |          |
|      |               |       |          |       |          |
|      |               |       |          |       |          |

# THE PACKET ASSIGNMENTS CHART

| Page | Line/Measures | Tempo | Due Date | Notes | Achieved |
|------|---------------|-------|----------|-------|----------|
|      |               |       |          |       |          |
|      |               |       |          |       |          |
|      |               |       |          |       |          |
|      |               |       |          |       |          |
|      |               |       |          |       |          |
|      |               |       |          |       |          |
|      |               |       |          |       |          |
|      |               |       |          |       |          |
|      |               |       |          |       |          |
|      |               |       |          |       |          |
|      |               |       |          |       |          |
|      |               |       |          |       |          |
|      |               |       |          |       |          |
|      |               |       |          |       |          |
|      |               |       |          |       |          |
|      |               |       |          |       |          |
|      |               |       |          |       |          |
|      |               |       |          |       |          |
|      |               |       |          |       |          |
|      |               |       |          |       |          |
|      |               |       |          |       |          |
|      |               |       |          |       |          |
|      |               |       |          |       |          |
|      |               |       |          |       |          |
|      |               |       |          |       |          |
|      |               |       |          |       |          |
|      |               |       |          |       |          |
|      |               |       |          |       |          |
|      |               |       |          |       |          |
|      |               |       |          |       |          |
|      |               |       |          |       |          |
|      |               |       |          |       |          |
|      |               |       |          |       |          |
|      |               |       |          |       |          |
|      |               |       |          |       |          |
|      |               |       |          |       |          |
|      |               |       |          |       |          |
|      |               |       |          |       |          |
|      |               |       |          |       |          |
|      |               |       |          |       |          |
|      |               |       |          |       |          |
|      |               |       |          |       |          |

# The Packet Assignments Chart

| Page | Line/Measures | Tempo | Due Date | Notes | Achieved |
|------|---------------|-------|----------|-------|----------|
|      |               |       |          |       |          |
|      |               |       |          |       |          |
|      |               |       |          |       |          |
|      |               |       |          |       |          |
|      |               |       |          |       |          |
|      |               |       |          |       |          |
|      |               |       |          |       |          |
|      |               |       |          |       |          |
|      |               |       |          |       |          |
|      |               |       |          |       |          |
|      |               |       |          |       |          |
|      |               |       |          |       |          |
|      |               |       |          |       |          |
|      |               |       |          |       |          |
|      |               |       |          |       |          |
|      |               |       |          |       |          |
|      |               |       |          |       |          |
|      |               |       |          |       |          |
|      |               |       |          |       |          |
|      |               |       |          |       |          |
|      |               |       |          |       |          |
|      |               |       |          |       |          |
|      |               |       |          |       |          |
|      |               |       |          |       |          |
|      |               |       |          |       |          |
|      |               |       |          |       |          |
|      |               |       |          |       |          |
|      |               |       |          |       |          |
|      |               |       |          |       |          |
|      |               |       |          |       |          |
|      |               |       |          |       |          |
|      |               |       |          |       |          |
|      |               |       |          |       |          |
|      |               |       |          |       |          |
|      |               |       |          |       |          |
|      |               |       |          |       |          |
|      |               |       |          |       |          |
|      |               |       |          |       |          |
|      |               |       |          |       |          |
|      |               |       |          |       |          |

# The Packet Assignments Chart

| Page | Line/Measures | Tempo | Due Date | Notes | Achieved |
|------|---------------|-------|----------|-------|----------|
|      |               |       |          |       |          |
|      |               |       |          |       |          |
|      |               |       |          |       |          |
|      |               |       |          |       |          |
|      |               |       |          |       |          |
|      |               |       |          |       |          |
|      |               |       |          |       |          |
|      |               |       |          |       |          |
|      |               |       |          |       |          |
|      |               |       |          |       |          |
|      |               |       |          |       |          |
|      |               |       |          |       |          |
|      |               |       |          |       |          |
|      |               |       |          |       |          |
|      |               |       |          |       |          |
|      |               |       |          |       |          |
|      |               |       |          |       |          |
|      |               |       |          |       |          |
|      |               |       |          |       |          |
|      |               |       |          |       |          |
|      |               |       |          |       |          |
|      |               |       |          |       |          |
|      |               |       |          |       |          |
|      |               |       |          |       |          |
|      |               |       |          |       |          |
|      |               |       |          |       |          |
|      |               |       |          |       |          |
|      |               |       |          |       |          |
|      |               |       |          |       |          |
|      |               |       |          |       |          |
|      |               |       |          |       |          |
|      |               |       |          |       |          |
|      |               |       |          |       |          |
|      |               |       |          |       |          |
|      |               |       |          |       |          |
|      |               |       |          |       |          |
|      |               |       |          |       |          |
|      |               |       |          |       |          |
|      |               |       |          |       |          |
|      |               |       |          |       |          |

# The Packet Assignments Chart

| Page | Line/Measures | Tempo | Due Date | Notes | Achieved |
|---|---|---|---|---|---|
| | | | | | |
| | | | | | |
| | | | | | |
| | | | | | |
| | | | | | |
| | | | | | |
| | | | | | |
| | | | | | |
| | | | | | |
| | | | | | |
| | | | | | |
| | | | | | |
| | | | | | |
| | | | | | |
| | | | | | |
| | | | | | |
| | | | | | |
| | | | | | |
| | | | | | |
| | | | | | |
| | | | | | |
| | | | | | |
| | | | | | |
| | | | | | |
| | | | | | |
| | | | | | |
| | | | | | |
| | | | | | |
| | | | | | |
| | | | | | |
| | | | | | |
| | | | | | |
| | | | | | |
| | | | | | |
| | | | | | |
| | | | | | |
| | | | | | |
| | | | | | |
| | | | | | |
| | | | | | |
| | | | | | |

# The Packet Assignments Chart

| Page | Line/Measures | Tempo | Due Date | Notes | Achieved |
|------|---------------|-------|----------|-------|----------|
|  |  |  |  |  |  |
|  |  |  |  |  |  |
|  |  |  |  |  |  |
|  |  |  |  |  |  |
|  |  |  |  |  |  |
|  |  |  |  |  |  |
|  |  |  |  |  |  |
|  |  |  |  |  |  |
|  |  |  |  |  |  |
|  |  |  |  |  |  |
|  |  |  |  |  |  |
|  |  |  |  |  |  |
|  |  |  |  |  |  |
|  |  |  |  |  |  |
|  |  |  |  |  |  |
|  |  |  |  |  |  |
|  |  |  |  |  |  |
|  |  |  |  |  |  |
|  |  |  |  |  |  |
|  |  |  |  |  |  |
|  |  |  |  |  |  |
|  |  |  |  |  |  |
|  |  |  |  |  |  |
|  |  |  |  |  |  |
|  |  |  |  |  |  |
|  |  |  |  |  |  |
|  |  |  |  |  |  |
|  |  |  |  |  |  |
|  |  |  |  |  |  |
|  |  |  |  |  |  |
|  |  |  |  |  |  |
|  |  |  |  |  |  |
|  |  |  |  |  |  |
|  |  |  |  |  |  |
|  |  |  |  |  |  |
|  |  |  |  |  |  |
|  |  |  |  |  |  |
|  |  |  |  |  |  |
|  |  |  |  |  |  |
|  |  |  |  |  |  |
|  |  |  |  |  |  |

# The Packet Assignments Chart

| Page | Line/Measures | Tempo | Due Date | Notes | Achieved |
|------|---------------|-------|----------|-------|----------|
|      |               |       |          |       |          |
|      |               |       |          |       |          |
|      |               |       |          |       |          |
|      |               |       |          |       |          |
|      |               |       |          |       |          |
|      |               |       |          |       |          |
|      |               |       |          |       |          |
|      |               |       |          |       |          |
|      |               |       |          |       |          |
|      |               |       |          |       |          |
|      |               |       |          |       |          |
|      |               |       |          |       |          |
|      |               |       |          |       |          |
|      |               |       |          |       |          |
|      |               |       |          |       |          |
|      |               |       |          |       |          |
|      |               |       |          |       |          |
|      |               |       |          |       |          |
|      |               |       |          |       |          |
|      |               |       |          |       |          |
|      |               |       |          |       |          |
|      |               |       |          |       |          |
|      |               |       |          |       |          |
|      |               |       |          |       |          |
|      |               |       |          |       |          |
|      |               |       |          |       |          |
|      |               |       |          |       |          |
|      |               |       |          |       |          |
|      |               |       |          |       |          |
|      |               |       |          |       |          |
|      |               |       |          |       |          |
|      |               |       |          |       |          |
|      |               |       |          |       |          |
|      |               |       |          |       |          |
|      |               |       |          |       |          |
|      |               |       |          |       |          |
|      |               |       |          |       |          |
|      |               |       |          |       |          |
|      |               |       |          |       |          |

# The Packet Assignments Chart

| Page | Line/Measures | Tempo | Due Date | Notes | Achieved |
|------|---------------|-------|----------|-------|----------|
|      |               |       |          |       |          |
|      |               |       |          |       |          |
|      |               |       |          |       |          |
|      |               |       |          |       |          |
|      |               |       |          |       |          |
|      |               |       |          |       |          |
|      |               |       |          |       |          |
|      |               |       |          |       |          |
|      |               |       |          |       |          |
|      |               |       |          |       |          |
|      |               |       |          |       |          |
|      |               |       |          |       |          |
|      |               |       |          |       |          |
|      |               |       |          |       |          |
|      |               |       |          |       |          |
|      |               |       |          |       |          |
|      |               |       |          |       |          |
|      |               |       |          |       |          |
|      |               |       |          |       |          |
|      |               |       |          |       |          |
|      |               |       |          |       |          |
|      |               |       |          |       |          |
|      |               |       |          |       |          |
|      |               |       |          |       |          |
|      |               |       |          |       |          |
|      |               |       |          |       |          |
|      |               |       |          |       |          |
|      |               |       |          |       |          |
|      |               |       |          |       |          |
|      |               |       |          |       |          |
|      |               |       |          |       |          |
|      |               |       |          |       |          |
|      |               |       |          |       |          |
|      |               |       |          |       |          |
|      |               |       |          |       |          |
|      |               |       |          |       |          |
|      |               |       |          |       |          |
|      |               |       |          |       |          |
|      |               |       |          |       |          |

# The Packet Assignments Chart

| Page | Line/Measures | Tempo | Due Date | Notes | Achieved |
|------|---------------|-------|----------|-------|----------|
|      |               |       |          |       |          |
|      |               |       |          |       |          |
|      |               |       |          |       |          |
|      |               |       |          |       |          |
|      |               |       |          |       |          |
|      |               |       |          |       |          |
|      |               |       |          |       |          |
|      |               |       |          |       |          |
|      |               |       |          |       |          |
|      |               |       |          |       |          |
|      |               |       |          |       |          |
|      |               |       |          |       |          |
|      |               |       |          |       |          |
|      |               |       |          |       |          |
|      |               |       |          |       |          |
|      |               |       |          |       |          |
|      |               |       |          |       |          |
|      |               |       |          |       |          |
|      |               |       |          |       |          |
|      |               |       |          |       |          |
|      |               |       |          |       |          |
|      |               |       |          |       |          |
|      |               |       |          |       |          |
|      |               |       |          |       |          |
|      |               |       |          |       |          |
|      |               |       |          |       |          |
|      |               |       |          |       |          |
|      |               |       |          |       |          |
|      |               |       |          |       |          |
|      |               |       |          |       |          |
|      |               |       |          |       |          |
|      |               |       |          |       |          |
|      |               |       |          |       |          |
|      |               |       |          |       |          |
|      |               |       |          |       |          |
|      |               |       |          |       |          |
|      |               |       |          |       |          |
|      |               |       |          |       |          |
|      |               |       |          |       |          |

# The Packet Assignments Chart

| Page | Line/Measures | Tempo | Due Date | Notes | Achieved |
|------|---------------|-------|----------|-------|----------|
|      |               |       |          |       |          |
|      |               |       |          |       |          |
|      |               |       |          |       |          |
|      |               |       |          |       |          |
|      |               |       |          |       |          |
|      |               |       |          |       |          |
|      |               |       |          |       |          |
|      |               |       |          |       |          |
|      |               |       |          |       |          |
|      |               |       |          |       |          |
|      |               |       |          |       |          |
|      |               |       |          |       |          |
|      |               |       |          |       |          |
|      |               |       |          |       |          |
|      |               |       |          |       |          |
|      |               |       |          |       |          |
|      |               |       |          |       |          |
|      |               |       |          |       |          |
|      |               |       |          |       |          |
|      |               |       |          |       |          |
|      |               |       |          |       |          |
|      |               |       |          |       |          |
|      |               |       |          |       |          |
|      |               |       |          |       |          |
|      |               |       |          |       |          |
|      |               |       |          |       |          |
|      |               |       |          |       |          |
|      |               |       |          |       |          |
|      |               |       |          |       |          |
|      |               |       |          |       |          |
|      |               |       |          |       |          |
|      |               |       |          |       |          |
|      |               |       |          |       |          |
|      |               |       |          |       |          |
|      |               |       |          |       |          |
|      |               |       |          |       |          |
|      |               |       |          |       |          |
|      |               |       |          |       |          |
|      |               |       |          |       |          |
|      |               |       |          |       |          |
|      |               |       |          |       |          |
|      |               |       |          |       |          |
|      |               |       |          |       |          |

# THE PACKET ASSIGNMENTS CHART

| Page | Line/Measures | Tempo | Due Date | Notes | Achieved |
|------|---------------|-------|----------|-------|----------|
|  |  |  |  |  |  |
|  |  |  |  |  |  |
|  |  |  |  |  |  |
|  |  |  |  |  |  |
|  |  |  |  |  |  |
|  |  |  |  |  |  |
|  |  |  |  |  |  |
|  |  |  |  |  |  |
|  |  |  |  |  |  |
|  |  |  |  |  |  |
|  |  |  |  |  |  |
|  |  |  |  |  |  |
|  |  |  |  |  |  |
|  |  |  |  |  |  |
|  |  |  |  |  |  |
|  |  |  |  |  |  |
|  |  |  |  |  |  |
|  |  |  |  |  |  |
|  |  |  |  |  |  |
|  |  |  |  |  |  |
|  |  |  |  |  |  |
|  |  |  |  |  |  |
|  |  |  |  |  |  |
|  |  |  |  |  |  |
|  |  |  |  |  |  |
|  |  |  |  |  |  |
|  |  |  |  |  |  |
|  |  |  |  |  |  |
|  |  |  |  |  |  |
|  |  |  |  |  |  |
|  |  |  |  |  |  |
|  |  |  |  |  |  |
|  |  |  |  |  |  |
|  |  |  |  |  |  |
|  |  |  |  |  |  |
|  |  |  |  |  |  |
|  |  |  |  |  |  |
|  |  |  |  |  |  |
|  |  |  |  |  |  |

# The Packet Assignments Chart

| Page | Line/Measures | Tempo | Due Date | Notes | Achieved |
|------|---------------|-------|----------|-------|----------|
|      |               |       |          |       |          |
|      |               |       |          |       |          |
|      |               |       |          |       |          |
|      |               |       |          |       |          |
|      |               |       |          |       |          |
|      |               |       |          |       |          |
|      |               |       |          |       |          |
|      |               |       |          |       |          |
|      |               |       |          |       |          |
|      |               |       |          |       |          |
|      |               |       |          |       |          |
|      |               |       |          |       |          |
|      |               |       |          |       |          |
|      |               |       |          |       |          |
|      |               |       |          |       |          |
|      |               |       |          |       |          |
|      |               |       |          |       |          |
|      |               |       |          |       |          |
|      |               |       |          |       |          |
|      |               |       |          |       |          |
|      |               |       |          |       |          |
|      |               |       |          |       |          |
|      |               |       |          |       |          |
|      |               |       |          |       |          |
|      |               |       |          |       |          |
|      |               |       |          |       |          |
|      |               |       |          |       |          |
|      |               |       |          |       |          |
|      |               |       |          |       |          |
|      |               |       |          |       |          |
|      |               |       |          |       |          |
|      |               |       |          |       |          |
|      |               |       |          |       |          |
|      |               |       |          |       |          |
|      |               |       |          |       |          |
|      |               |       |          |       |          |
|      |               |       |          |       |          |
|      |               |       |          |       |          |
|      |               |       |          |       |          |

# The Packet Assignments Chart

| Page | Line/Measures | Tempo | Due Date | Notes | Achieved |
|------|---------------|-------|----------|-------|----------|
|      |               |       |          |       |          |
|      |               |       |          |       |          |
|      |               |       |          |       |          |
|      |               |       |          |       |          |
|      |               |       |          |       |          |
|      |               |       |          |       |          |
|      |               |       |          |       |          |
|      |               |       |          |       |          |
|      |               |       |          |       |          |
|      |               |       |          |       |          |
|      |               |       |          |       |          |
|      |               |       |          |       |          |
|      |               |       |          |       |          |
|      |               |       |          |       |          |
|      |               |       |          |       |          |
|      |               |       |          |       |          |
|      |               |       |          |       |          |
|      |               |       |          |       |          |
|      |               |       |          |       |          |
|      |               |       |          |       |          |
|      |               |       |          |       |          |
|      |               |       |          |       |          |
|      |               |       |          |       |          |
|      |               |       |          |       |          |
|      |               |       |          |       |          |
|      |               |       |          |       |          |
|      |               |       |          |       |          |
|      |               |       |          |       |          |
|      |               |       |          |       |          |
|      |               |       |          |       |          |
|      |               |       |          |       |          |
|      |               |       |          |       |          |
|      |               |       |          |       |          |
|      |               |       |          |       |          |
|      |               |       |          |       |          |
|      |               |       |          |       |          |
|      |               |       |          |       |          |
|      |               |       |          |       |          |
|      |               |       |          |       |          |
|      |               |       |          |       |          |

# THE PACKET ASSIGNMENTS CHART

| Page | Line/Measures | Tempo | Due Date | Notes | Achieved |
|------|---------------|-------|----------|-------|----------|
|      |               |       |          |       |          |
|      |               |       |          |       |          |
|      |               |       |          |       |          |
|      |               |       |          |       |          |
|      |               |       |          |       |          |
|      |               |       |          |       |          |
|      |               |       |          |       |          |
|      |               |       |          |       |          |
|      |               |       |          |       |          |
|      |               |       |          |       |          |
|      |               |       |          |       |          |
|      |               |       |          |       |          |
|      |               |       |          |       |          |
|      |               |       |          |       |          |
|      |               |       |          |       |          |
|      |               |       |          |       |          |
|      |               |       |          |       |          |
|      |               |       |          |       |          |
|      |               |       |          |       |          |
|      |               |       |          |       |          |
|      |               |       |          |       |          |
|      |               |       |          |       |          |
|      |               |       |          |       |          |
|      |               |       |          |       |          |
|      |               |       |          |       |          |
|      |               |       |          |       |          |
|      |               |       |          |       |          |
|      |               |       |          |       |          |
|      |               |       |          |       |          |
|      |               |       |          |       |          |
|      |               |       |          |       |          |
|      |               |       |          |       |          |
|      |               |       |          |       |          |
|      |               |       |          |       |          |
|      |               |       |          |       |          |
|      |               |       |          |       |          |
|      |               |       |          |       |          |
|      |               |       |          |       |          |
|      |               |       |          |       |          |
|      |               |       |          |       |          |
|      |               |       |          |       |          |